Psychological Debriefing
A Leader's Guide
For Small Group Crisis Intervention

Atle Dyregrov, Ph.D.

CHEVRON
PUBLISHING CORPORATION

Printed in the United States of America

ISBN: 1-883581-31-1

FIRST AMERICAN EDITION
© 2003 Chevron Publishing Corporation

First published in Norwegian as
Psykologisk Debriefing
by Fagbokforlaget, Bergen (2002)

CHEVRON
PUBLISHING CORPORATION
5018 Dorsey Hall Drive, Suite 104
Ellicott City, MD 21042
410-740-0065

Biographical Sketch

ATLE DYREGROV, Ph.D.

Dr. Atle Dyregrov is the director of the Center for Crisis Psychology in Bergen, Norway. He is a clinical and research psychologist, holding memberships in the Norwegian Psychological Association as well as an associate membership in the American Psychological Association. He is a board member of the International Critical Incident Stress Foundation and one of the founders of the European Society for Traumatic Stress Studies. He lectures both on the Faculty of Medicine and Faculty of Psychology at Bergen University. His former experience includes four years of clinical and research work at the Children's Hospital in Bergen, and four years at the University of Bergen. He has been the director for the Center for Crisis Psychology since its formation in 1988.

Dr. Dyregrov is the author of numerous publications, journal articles, and books including "Grief in Children" published in nine languages, "Disaster Psychology," "Grief and Care Within Schools" (co-authored with Magne Raudalen), "Children and War" (co-authored with Magne Raudalen), and "Children on the Intensive Care Unit" (with several other authors). His book on sleep, "The Little Sleep Book," was published in Norwegian in 2001 and also in other Scandinavian languages. His book titled "Psychological Debriefing: A Leader's Guide for Small Group Crisis Intervention" was published in Norwegian in 2002.

Dr. Dyregrov has lectured extensively in the Scandinavian countries, as well as in Europe and the U.S. He has worked as a consultant to different U.N. organizations, especially with UNICEF in their work for children in war in Africa, the Middle

East, and former Yugoslavia, and with UNHCR in developing staff support routines around the world.

His clinical work has covered areas such as: grief reactions in parents following the loss of a child, grief and trauma in children, organizing psychosocial disaster assistance, critical incident stress debriefing for disaster workers, and children in war situations.

Contents

Chapter 4

Chapter 5

Chapter 6

Chapter 7

Chapter 8

Chapter 9

References

Foreword

I welcome with delight and exhilaration the publication of Atle Dyregrov's book, *Psychological Debriefing: A Leader's Guide To Small Group Crisis Intervention.* The arrival of this special book has been long anticipated. *Psychological Debriefing* will surely make a memorable positive mark on the field of crisis intervention. I am certain that it will enhance the group tactics in CISM. Any crisis interventionist will benefit from this well-written text which is based upon sound theory, careful research, and the author's many years of real world experience in providing individual and group crisis intervention and trauma management services.

Few people may realize just how significant this contribution from Dr. Dyregrov really is. *Psychological Debriefing*'s publication signals the beginning of a new era of maturity for CISM in which innovative authors in the CISM field will bring new ideas and insights generated by their own backgrounds and experiences. Their knowledge contributes to the field by encouraging people to think more attentively about the manner in which they apply their crisis intervention skills. Fresh ideas enhance the refinement of this growing field. They help to make crisis intervention a more solid, more careful, more precise, and a more adaptable system of support services.

Dr. Dyregrov brings his own style to the field. As a result of cultural considerations and personal preferences, his management of debriefings may vary somewhat from what is done in the U.S. The concepts and suggestions he presents, however, are based upon the same core crisis intervention principles as CISD and the other group processes within CISM. Dr. Dyregrov and I have worked together both in team teaching crisis intervention concepts and in providing small group crisis intervention services in Norway and in the U.S. We have blended our small group interventions together into a seamless fit. Aspects of both of our styles have been helpful to those in a state of crisis. We have learned from each other and our styles have positively influenced one another.

Psychological Debriefing is filled from cover to cover with interesting and thoughtful material. A serious reading of the material helps one to appreciate more than ever the complexity of providing small group crisis interventions to traumatized people. The book warns of the dangers of inadequately-trained CISM personnel and the lack of effective standards of practice. It is clearly stated in the book's chapters that many factors must be blended together by a skillful team in order to assure successful small group interventions. Timing, leadership, the nature of the traumatic event, the nature of the group, the atmosphere of the organization, and the skill of the team members are among the many other factors that must be considered, planned for, and responded to every time a debriefing process is applied. Each chapter provides essential details, subtle insights into group processes, and specific guidelines that can augment previous crisis intervention training.

Atle Dyregrov's experience is extensive. He has served in multiple war zones including Iraq, Palestine, Uganda and Rwanda. His skills have been further honed in numerous disasters on several continents. Dr. Dyregrov has been involved in assisting victims and family members to recover from violent episodes, child murders, bombings, mass murders, and the sinking of a ferry boat with a great loss of lives. He has worked with emergency personnel, the military, corporations, the United Nations, communities, and schools. He brings a special expertise to CISM in that he is a world-renowned expert in the field of children's trauma. Dr. Dyregrov is the director of the Center for Crisis Psychology in Bergen, Norway. He is a teacher with exceptional skills. His research is impeccable. His writings have been applauded around the world. His understanding of human pain and his compassion, warmth, and kindness go well beyond that of the average person.

Psychological Debriefing: A Leader's Guide To Small Group Crisis Intervention needed to be written and it needed to be written by Atle Dyregrov. I cannot think of anyone who could have brought more knowledge and experience into the project or who could have accomplished a more outstanding job on the topic. I offer my deepest appreciation for his dedicated work on *Psychological Debriefing*. The reader now has a chance to learn from a true master of crisis intervention. I applaud his contribution and welcome it with enthusiasm.

Atle Dyregrov is my colleague, my teacher, and a charismatic leader who has made many previous contributions to CISM. But, most importantly he is my friend!

Jeffrey T. Mitchell, PhD, CTS
President, ICISF
November 2002

Preface

From the start, I have meant this book to be a practical workbook that focused on the processes involved in psychological debriefings. Its purpose, therefore, is to help leaders conduct effective small group interventions for people who have experienced sudden, dramatic events. However, some mention of what this book is *not* about is appropriate at the outset. The reader of this book cannot go out and conduct effective group debriefing by merely reading this book. This book can never replace the training and experience that is required to conduct good debriefings. In order to do so it is essential to have attended a well-designed training exercise that involves the participants in role-plays where one can get a better understanding of the processes involved and how to handle them. In addition, a debriefing leader needs solid knowledge of short-term and long-term crisis reactions. With practice, good leadership skills will grow and gradually, it will become possible to conduct more effective meetings.

This book does not set out to describe all the major tasks in setting up integrated Critical Incident Stress Management (CISM) programs, nor does it depict the risks involved when such programs are not properly established, run, and monitored. For such issues the reader is referred to Mitchell and Everly (2001). The literature written by these two colleagues expands and provides elaboration on many of the themes that are only briefly described or discussed in this book. Although some of the same principles are useful in group debriefings for children, this book is primarily about how such meetings can be facilitated for adults (for a discussion of debriefing used with children see Wraith, 1995, 1997, 2000).

Acknowledgments

Over the past 20 years, many people have served to influence my thinking and practice of small group crisis intervention (psychological debriefings and defusings).

First and foremost is Jeffrey T. Mitchell. When I attended a presentation by Jeffrey in 1981, he described the Critical Incident Stress Debriefing (CISD) model. I quickly noted the similarity to my approach for families who had lost children and saw its potential for assisting Norwegian helpers of various categories. Since then, Jeff's writing, our many conversations, and the deep friendship that has evolved has meant much for my own professional development. Although we have our different views, the basic model at the heart of my own approach has been adapted from Jeff. I am forever indebted to him for his inspiration and friendship.

Internationally, Robyn Robinson in Australia, Roger Solomon in the U.S., William Yule, Gordon Turnbull and Stephen Regel in the U.K., Soili Poijula in Finland, and Gerry Larsson and Rolf Glavmo in Sweden have influenced my thinking and work. My gratitude goes to them all.

In Norway, Magne Raundalen has been my mentor, colleague, and friend. I do not know of anyone more intellectually generous than Magne. For children, parents (caregivers), and helpers involved in war situations around the globe, he has developed ingenious ways of helping and has been instrumental in introducing procedures that include debriefings adapted to such situations.

Odd H. Hellesøy, another mentor of mine, provided me with the opportunities to pursue my interest in this area. His background in psychiatry and social medicine has given him a broad perspective that, coupled with his reflective mind, have helped me develop and critically review different areas within crisis intervention and trauma care.

Jakob Inge Kristoffersen, my co-founder of the Center for Crisis Psychology, is one of the most skilled clinicians and debriefers that I know. During the first years of the Center's operation, we had plenty of possibilities to work together during debriefings and to alternate the leadership. During discussions before and after the debriefings, we refined ideas and tried them out or reflected more on them as new debriefings were conducted. During team teaching about debriefing throughout Scandinavia and in other parts of the world (for the United Nations), ideas were developed to the point where we sometimes did not recall who had the original thought or suggestion. Therefore, to some extent, part of what is written here is owed to Jakki (as we call him).

Other members of the staff at the Center for Crisis Psychology, Elin, Marianne, and Rolf, to mention a few, have also contributed in various ways. Through our weekly professional meetings where debriefing has been an often-discussed theme, opinions are melded, recreated, altered, or built. This is the building block of practice and good interaction. Lastly, but very importantly, my wife Kari, also a member of our staff, has been a sparring partner for discussions where her sharp mind coupled with her insight in human nature as well as her professional capacity (as a sociologist and a physiotherapist) have been invaluable.

I am also indebted to my good friend Bill (William) Yule from The Institute of Psychiatry in London. His sharp and resourceful mind has helped me rethink my own impressions and inter-pretations of various phenomena related to debriefing. Also Stephen Regel, who is now director of the Centre for Trauma Studies in Nottingham, England, has been helpful in discussing various aspects of debriefing. Having co-taught seminars with him, I have learned from his vast experience in using debriefing in various fields. Last, but not least, a good friend and colleague, Dr. Gordon Turnbull, from the Traumatic Stress Unit at Ticehurst House Hospital in England, has inspired me through this work. He also helped by reading through this manuscript to improve my English, although the responsibility for all mistakes and awkward sentences lies with me.

The many participants who have attended courses I have led on training for psychological debriefing have contributed through numerous role-plays where we have had a chance to study processes in detail through video-filmed scenarios. This has been of invaluable help in understanding how the different approaches taken by leaders and different leadership styles have unique consequences for the group. This has made dissection of aspects of the group process possible. These participants deserve a "thank you" for their willingness to be part of scenarios even though it may have been stressful at times.

1

Groups and Critical Incidents

The Use of Groups Following Critical Incidents

Before aspects of psychological debriefing are described in more detail, let us remind ourselves about why so many people find it helpful to meet with others following critical events. In his groundbreaking work on group therapy, Irving Yalom (1970) discussed the beneficial elements active in therapeutic groups. Many of those same beneficial elements are applicable to the present discussion. They include the opportunity:

- To have a chance to put into words the different aspects of one's experience
- To have a chance to obtain facts from others who experienced the same event
- To be able to help others by providing facts, support, or a "listening ear"
- To understand the reasons why others behaved as they did
- To develop alternative perspectives
- To learn what others do to cope with the event and get ideas on what to do
- To learn information about normal reactions to critical events and having one's reactions affirmed by others
- To gain specific advice on how to handle intrusive memories, sleep disturbances, etc.
- To reduce the stigma of getting help
- To be screened for further referral if needed

People have the opportunity to structure their experience in groups. Together, with others who experienced the same event, they can integrate their own perspective to establish a more complete appreciation of their experience. Participants are given early opportunities to put words to their experience, including thoughts, impressions, and reactions, as well as accessing peer support; and they can develop a more collective perspective. Group psychological debriefings are believed to lead to structuring of crisis experiences, linking together the different experiences and perspectives of the individual group members into a whole. At the same time, they demonstrate to participants the caring role of their organizations or their communities.

Necessary Ingredients For Effective Crisis Groups

When a group is to be formed following a critical event, some important aspects must be addressed.

There must be:

- Participant motivation
- An expressed need from participants
- Knowledgeable leadership
- Structure and rules
- Respect among participants
- Investment of energy from the leaders
- A leader knowledgeable of stress reactions, coping resources, and group dynamics
- "Cultural" knowledge within the group

It is obvious that most of the responsibility for making groups work is placed on the leaders. Nevertheless, it is important not to try to use such groups if the event has only had a marginal effect on participants. If the group has already spent considerable time discussing the event, they may suffer from lack of motivation to participate, as they intuitively doubt that the debriefing meeting will be significantly different from the conversations they already may have had. At such times the debriefing leaders have to motivate participants by pointing out that the debriefing will be more structured, contain more information, and therefore be quite different from an informal conversation.

Structure is important in all groups. In therapy groups, meetings are spread over many weeks or months to achieve the desired outcome; in debriefing groups, there are only hours available to achieve group goals. Rohde and Stockton (1994) emphasize the importance of structure in group meetings, although they warn against the possibility of too much structure. Structure is provided by:

- Clear procedures for the timing of meetings
- The physical environment
- Clearly-stated purposes
- Directive leadership
- Structure during the meeting
- Clear expectations for what will happen, i.e., explicit explanations of the sequence of procedures.

Yalom (1995) wrote, "Anxiety is relieved when one is provided with clear, firm expectations for behavior in a new situation" (p. 468). If a group has previously experienced psychological debriefings, then the structure can be relaxed because the participants will know what to expect. Throughout this book I emphasize how leaders can use the group itself to stimulate its own intrinsic process. Without proper training, background, or experience, it is hard to achieve this. Just as debriefing leaders should try to learn as much as they can about the "culture" of the group they are going to meet, they have to invest time in improving their group-handling skills.

2

Group Psychological Debriefing

Terminology

Throughout this book I will use the shorter word **debriefing** instead of the longer term **"group psychological debriefing"** for the structure and process followed in meetings that usually last between two and three hours. The term is not used for individual one-to-one meetings, but for the formal, structured discussion in groups of the facts, thoughts, impressions, and reactions related to a critical event. This meeting usually takes place on one of the first few days following the event, while a meeting on the same day as the event is denoted as a **defusing** (see Mitchell & Everly, 2001). I sometimes use the term "a first talk-through" to refer to these meetings for people outside the helping professions. In the U.S., Jeffrey T. Mitchell introduced the term "Critical Incident Stress Debriefing" or CISD meetings, as he found that emergency personnel were skeptical of everything with psychological connotations. Using the debriefing model for other groups outside emergency professions and also in a European cultural context, I have preferred to use the term "psychological debriefing." The use of the term "psychological" is to differentiate this process from the **"operational debriefing"** where actions taken are reviewed in order to learn from the experience. The focus of operational debriefing is on evaluating fulfillment of roles and functions, activities, procedures, and equipment.

Group psychological debriefings are held for ordinary people who experience normal reactions to abnormal events, and are part of crisis intervention. Unfortunately, sometimes they are regarded as a form of psychotherapy, which they are not, although they will have therapeutic value. When used as part of a focused strategy to help a group months later, they may assume more therapeutic effect following exposure to trauma (Chemtob, Law, Tomas & Cremniter, 1997; Mitchell, Schiller, Eyler & Everly, 1999).

Throughout the book, I refer to the psychiatric condition known as **posttraumatic stress disorder (PTSD)**. Although familiar to most readers, this term refers to a diagnosis made when the intensity and duration of reactions following a traumatic event converge to form a particular, enduring pattern. Apart from having lasted for a month, and following the experience of having witnessed or having been confronted with an event or events that involved actual or threatened death or serious injury or threat to the physical integrity of self or others, the criteria ensure that the emotional response must involve intense fear, helplessness, or horror. The diagnosis of PTSD requires: a) persistent re-experiencing of the event, b) persistent avoidance of stimuli associated with the trauma and numbing of general responsiveness, and c) persistent symptoms of increased arousal. The symptoms must cause clinically significant distress or impairment in social, occupational, or other important areas of functioning (DSM-IV: the Diagnostic & Statistical Manual of the American Psychiatric Association, Fourth Edition, 1994).

History of Group Debriefing

Jeffrey T. Mitchell and George S. Everly, Jr. (2001) wrote that the first rudimentary debriefings were undertaken on the beaches of France following the invasion of Normandy in World War II in 1944. The stress of the experience was of such a magnitude that military leaders gathered the invading soldiers in smaller groups to talk about it. Debriefing as a concept has been used in the military to denote the meetings held following a mission, briefing being the term for the pre-mission meeting. However, the use of the concept related to the talk of psychological aspects of an experience emerged in the late 1970s and 1980s and has thereafter been used frequently.

Along with the military tradition for using meetings to assist personnel, several almost coincidental disasters triggered interest in this area: an Australian rail disaster, (the Granville train disaster outside Melbourne in 1977), and two plane crashes, one near San Diego in 1978 and another one outside Chicago in 1979. Beverly Raphael, an Australian psychiatrist, described the use of psychological debriefings for psychosocial helpers following the train disaster (1986); and Freeman (1979), Wagner (1979a,b) and others (Mitchell & Everly, 2001) described how interventions were organized to help emergency workers and police following plane crashes.

In addition to the historical use of debriefings following disasters, debriefings were also used in law enforcement, fire, and emergency medical personnel following involvement in critical events. Wagner (1979a,b) was one of the first to use systematic talk-through for police personnel involved in events such as shootings and other critical or life-threatening events. However, Jeffrey T. Mitchell was the first person to describe the use of the group format. In his capacity as a volunteer firefighter and graduate in psychology, he saw the need to instigate an improved care system for personnel following exposure to critical events. During the late 1970s he used a variety of different group formats to find the best one for emergency personnel. In 1983 he presented his structured Critical Incident Stress Debriefing (CISD) model for debriefing. This model has largely been adapted throughout the world for use in debriefings. The phases involved in his model were the introduction, fact, thought, reaction, symptom, teaching, and re-entry phase (Mitchell, 1983). Later in this book I describe these phases in more detail, although phrased slightly different. From the very beginning, debriefing was not meant to be the only intervention initiated to help personnel following a critical event.

Gradually the term **"Critical Incident Stress Management"** **(CISM)** (Everly & Mitchell, 1999) was used as the term to describe an integrated variety of care strategies used, such as pre-crisis education when possible, mobilization of peer, family, and organizational support, leader support, and individual follow-up and referral mechanisms for further assessment and therapy.

When Jeffrey T. Mitchell described the structure of de-briefings, it was primarily for use with emergency responders and based on experience from the North American continent. It is important to remember that the method was developed for use among predominantly male groups. The structure depicts a way that helps men express and recognize how stressful events may impact them, starting with what everybody can talk about (i.e., facts) and then gradually moving towards areas of experience (i.e., emotions) that men traditionally have sanctions against expressing. The structure and format have, however, been found useful in settings outside the emergency professions and outside primarily male settings. Adaptations of the Mitchell model have been proposed. However, variations of the Mitchell model continue to dominate the field as their usefulness of the model continues to be experienced by participants in debriefing groups. Although developed for helper groups, CISDs have not been used only for emergency responders, police, firefighters, and medical personnel. They also have been used for survivors of natural and man-made disasters, accidents, hostage and hijacking situations, violence and armed robbery, the death of a co-worker or friend, bystanders/witnesses, disaster victims, as well as to mediate organizational crisis and change.

What is a Group Psychological Debriefing?

A group psychological debriefing is a structured group meeting (discussion) organized for people to review in detail facts, thoughts, impressions, and reactions following a traumatic situation. Unfortunately, the term has been used for any kind of conversation or meeting held following a critical event, making it difficult to know what is meant by "a debriefing." This semantic problem has caused a great deal of unnecessary confusion and criticism regarding the usefulness of debriefing. A 15-minute informal conversation will be rather different than a structured meeting lasting 2½ hours.

The aims of such a structured meetings are to:

- Prevent unnecessary after-effects
- Accelerate normal recovery
- Stimulate group cohesion and support
- Maintain group spirit and motivation for living
- Promote a cognitive "grip" on the situation
- Stimulate emotional ventilation
- Normalize experience
- Screen those in need of further help.

Besides giving participants a chance to talk about experiences related to a more or less life-threatening or traumatic event, it also allows for expression of thoughts and reactions related to important losses that the participants have endured.

These meetings are not a form of psychotherapy but help to make sense of the experience in the early stages following a traumatic event or loss. They also provide group leaders with a chance to identify people who will need more extensive follow-up.

Debriefing meetings can be used for survivors of life-threatening events, i.e., non-injured survivors following transportation disasters, survivors of massacres, bereaved colleagues following a sudden death in the workplace, and for helpers following their involvement in situations that had a strong impact on them. This can include line of duty death or the suicide of a colleague, the death of a child resulting from violence or neglect, multiple casualty incidents, and major disasters. These are only some examples of the events for which debriefing meetings can be used. The structure of these meetings makes them easy to adjust to a variety of situations. However, such broad applicability of the format should lead to caution, and care should be taken not to overuse it for any difficult situation that a group has been through. This is not a process to mitigate the effects of burnout, or a stress management tool to be used following mildly upsetting events.

It is a process to be used for groups that: a) have worked with a severe stress or crisis event, or b) for groups that jointly have survived or experienced a life-threatening or severe situation (like the sudden unanticipated loss of a colleague).

The group psychological debriefing is part of the rubric of **early psychological intervention** and encompasses various efforts that are made to help people following exposure to a critical or traumatic event. Early interventions range from the comfort and care shown those who are admitted to hospitals following an injury, to more structured forms of psychological support provided in group settings, such as "psychological debriefings." These interventions belong to the domain of **"crisis intervention,"** aimed at reducing distress, stabilizing the situation, minimizing recovery time, and restoring function in individuals, families, and communities. The interventions used vary from setting to setting, from more formalized programs to secure follow-up for emergency personnel that deal with critical situations on an almost daily basis, e.g., Critical Incident Stress Management (Everly & Mitchell, 1999) to less structured interventions for people who suddenly are exposed to a traumatic event. Unfortunately the term "debriefing" has become a common term to describe both very brief early interventions and more elaborate practices.

Important measures included in early crisis intervention are: activation of good support and care from leaders in the organization or community; provision of information about the event(s) that took place; mobilization of support from family, friends and colleagues; individual follow-up for those in need; and information about helpful coping methods. Directly following a critical event, it may be advisable for affected people to gather in smaller groups to have a chance for an early talk-through (defusing), followed later by a more formal debriefing when necessary. A follow-up debriefing can be planned for three to five weeks later or earlier, if needed.

I think it is unlikely that people who experience highly stressful events will benefit from very short interventions (lasting less than an hour), and I do not see it as very humane to enter a family or person's life at a very vulnerable stage in their life, and then withdraw without proper follow-up. Such practice may be harmful.

Different Models of Debriefing

Over the years there have been a number of people who have come up with what they call different models of debriefing. However, my view is that most of these "new" models only are variations of Mitchell's original CISD model. These "new" models either apply debriefing in a different context or make some small adaptations to the model, or they de-emphasize one or some of the phases of the original model. An example is the "Multiple Stressor Debriefing Model" developed by Armstrong, O'Callahan, and Armstrong (1991) for debriefing Red Cross disaster personnel. This model has four stages: 1) disclosure of the event, 2) feelings and reactions, 3) coping strategies, and 4) termination. This model is intended to be used for situations where there may be no defined critical incident, but one where the rescue workers and helpers have been involved with an incident over an extended period of time, i.e., Red Cross personnel assisting following a disaster. The originators of the model emphasize that the groups seemed to function best with a group size limited to 12 to 15 members (as recommended in the process debriefings described in this book). They noted that the 1½ hour groups were too short and that visual aids to record stressors, feelings, and coping strategies were helpful in promoting the group to process their troubling events.

Shalev (2000) uses a "historical group debriefing" based on the work of S.L.A. Marshall, a U.S. army brigadier general in World War II. Here there is a systematic review of the event by all the participants, without advice, interpretation, or deliberate intervention. The length of the debriefing is similar to the type of debriefing recommended in this book. Shalev argues that to open up expression of emotion, making interpretations of response or description of symptoms may be inappropriate. There are important parallels to the model presented within this book, where interpretations are guarded against, and there is little focus on symptoms. However, in the debriefing format advocated herein, hearing about other people's reactions is essential to the process of normalizing reactions. In addition, much time is spent looking at cognitive impressions, to be able to draw on constructive thoughts and actions. However, in practice most process debriefings center on the actual history of the critical event and reactions are commented on but not dwelled upon. Especially with experienced groups such as emergency personnel, the format of historical group debriefing will be seen to be very similar to the format described in this book.

Some posttraumatic group interventions assume a very different form. Terr (1992) described what she termed "mini-marathon" groups as a first aid psychological intervention to use following disaster. These meetings last around three hours and are divided into three sections: story sharing, symptom sharing, and suggestions for self-help, including sharing tales of heroism and survival. In some respects it echoes what takes place in debriefings with primary victims, but in contrast with process debriefings, these meetings can include as many as 300 participants and continue with long meetings over several consecutive days. Although described 10 years ago, no studies have appeared to evaluate this intervention. My own experience is that smaller groups (less than 15) function best. I believe that this is because small groups make it possible for each participant to play a part and become involved. Just how important the element of personal involvement can be for trauma victims will be addressed later in this book. Armstrong et al. (1991) has particularly focused on the subject of personal involvement.

The Debriefing Debate

Given that the format of debriefing has been utilized with a wide variety of groups, it is not surprising that it has come under "the critical microscope." Recently, some studies and commentaries claim that psychological debriefings are of dubious benefit, and may actually increase problems (Deahl et al., 1994; Kenardy et al., 1996; Raphael, Meldrum & McFarlane, 1995). However, studies that report no effect of debriefing (or a negative effect, see Bisson, Jenkins, Alexander, & Bannister, 1997) have several methodological weaknesses:

- They analyze interventions that are called psychological debriefing but are actually single counseling sessions with medical patients.
- Several studies use self-selection to the intervention group and the control group.
- In some cases, it is not clearly defined what the debriefing actually consisted of.
- The timing of the intervention is variable and often outside the time period recommended.
- The intervention used seems to be clinically insufficient given the traumatic event experienced.
- The background and training of the persons who have carried out the interventions is unclear and possibly inadequate.
- The groups in the studies are not adequately matched.
- Debriefing is investigated in isolation, and not as part of an integrated continuum of assistance (e.g., CISM).

Although this book focuses on how to facilitate group debriefings, I strongly advocate the use of the debriefing intervention as one of several measures set in motion to care for people who experience a traumatic or critical incident. Other group activities include gathering together groups of victims to provide up-to-date information, and group therapy for those identified as being needful. CISM requires support from management or from community leaders, ample peer support, mobilization of family support, defusing, debriefing, and follow-up debriefing, ritualizations when appropriate, individual follow-up for those in need, and help in confronting situations that remind people of the critical event, i.e., returning to one's workplace following a violent situation at work. Richards (2001) found that following armed robbery, a structured CISM package of care produced superior outcome compared to a stand-alone CISD intervention. He found that employees in the CISM group were significantly less traumatized at later follow-up and that the number of clinically significant cases was less than half the number in the CISD alone group.

Self-selection is a particular problem in debriefing studies, because it must be presumed that persons who are characterized by avoidance and repression will avoid meetings where they are expected to talk about the event. First of all, those who do not feel the need for debriefing because they were peripheral to the event or felt that the event was of little consequence to them will refrain from debriefing and thus become part of the control group. Secondly, people who use avoidance and denial as a coping strategy will tend to stay away from such meetings. If such a "control" group were compared with a group that attends debriefings and has been encouraged to convert thoughts and reactions into words, then the debriefed group would be expected to yield higher scores on self-reported symptomatology. This may explain why some studies do not find positive effects for the intervention compared with the control group.

Saari, Lindeman, Verkasalo, and Prytz (1996) investigated crisis intervention provided for car ferry personnel on board a ferry that assisted during the rescue operation following the sinking of the ferry Estonia wherein 853 people lost their lives and 137 survived. They were unable to compare the debriefed and non-debriefed groups because those debriefed were more distressed at the outset. Those who participated in debriefing were more often found to have been eyewitnesses of the disaster. In addition, more women attended debriefing (women usually score higher on all symptom measures). Their results highlight difficult issues when comparing a debriefed group with a non-debriefed group when they have self-selected to the groups. Ursano, Fullerton, Vance, and Vang (2000) also found females significantly more likely to attend debriefings and the debriefed group to have been more exposed to a disaster than non-participants. My recent unpublished data have shown that survivors following a maritime disaster who opted to attend a debriefing had spent more time immersed in the sea and in the hospital. They also showed evidence of functional problems in their work, family, and private lives, compared with those who did not participate in the debriefing.

Nurmi (1999) studied helpers following the Estonia disaster and looked at posttraumatic stress reactions in several groups that were debriefed. These included rescue personnel, fire officers, police investigators, and disaster victim identification team members. A comparison study looked at these groups and a group of nurses that were not debriefed. On several measures the non-debriefed group evidenced significantly more reaction to the disaster and at very high levels. The nurses were the only all-female group.

A number of studies have concluded that psychological debriefing or CISD is followed by a positive effect for the participants (Bohl, 1991; Ford et al., 1993; Jenkins, 1996; Robinson & Mitchell, 1993; Stallard & Law, 1993; Yule & Udwin, 1991). Everly, Flannery & Mitchell (2000) have, in addition, reviewed a number of published and unpublished reports and case studies showing positive effects of debriefing. In almost all reports, including the negative studies previously described, when asked to rate their satisfaction or helpfulness, the participants of the debriefing groups (or individual meetings) experience the meetings as being helpful (Carlier, Voerman, & Gersons, 2000; Jenkins, 1996; Robinson & Mitchell, 1993; Turner, Thompson & Rosser, 1993). When Western Management Consultants conducted an independent evaluation of a CISM program for Canadian nurses working in isolated communities, they found the financial benefits of the service (e.g., reduction of costs associated with prevention of absenteeism and employee turnover) to be seven times greater than the cost of the service. In Australia a 60% decrease of costs related to armed robberies in a major Australian bank was reported following the instigation of a CISM program to support employees (Leeman-Conley, 1990). Tehrani (1995) reported that sick leave levels among employees who had been held in armed raids fell by 50% after the introduction of a multi-component trauma package. The text describes strategies that reduce the potential for acute stress reactions to traumatic exposure to "harden" into chronic and enduring reactions (such as PTSD). The package includes a model of individual intervention for victims in which the narrative description of the event is used to elicit more defined cognitive and emotional reactions (Tehrani & Westlake, 1994).

The studies mentioned above used other outcome measures than simple counting of PTSD or PTSD symptoms. Recently, Deahl and co-workers (2001) have questioned whether the right outcomes are being measured within debriefing research. For example, an outcome study involving British soldiers who had been deployed in peacekeeping operations in Bosnia indicated that the CISD intervention had the significant effect of reducing worrisome levels of alcohol misuse. The researchers recommended a broader range of outcome measures in future trials of debriefing. In addition to outcome measures such as sick leave, alcohol use, and the ability to function in work, a broader focus should include variables such as group morale and work motivation.

By far the most rigorously controlled studies into multi-component interventions have been undertaken by Flannery and his co-workers (Flannery, 1998; Flannery & Penk, 1996; Flannery, Fulton, Tausch, & Deloffi, 1991). They have used interventions including group debriefings, individual support, family counseling, and professional referral for staff following critical incidents within psychiatric hospitals. Once the program was in place there was less turnover, use of sick time, workers compensation claims, and medical and legal expenses. Even more astounding was the fact that there was a sharp decrease in the number of violent episodes following the instigation of the program.

Everly, Boyle and Lating (1999) conducted a meta-analysis based on group debriefing studies found in medical and psychological databases. They identified 14 empirical investigations of which 10 (sample size of 698) were utilized for the analysis. Three were excluded as they failed to use group-debriefing interventions and one because it failed to yield data that could be used meaningfully in the analysis. They found a significantly positive effect size (mean Cohen's d = .54, p < .01) resulting from the group debriefing intervention. The authors comment that this beneficial effect was revealed despite the wide variety of subject groups, the wide range of traumatic events, and the wide diversity of outcome measures. In an additional meta-analysis of the five investigations that had used the Mitchell specific group CISD-model of debriefing (with an aggregated sample size of 337), the mean Cohen's d was .86, indicative of a large positive effect attributable to the CISD intervention.

Many of the methodological objections raised in relation to the critical studies also are valid for the studies where positive results are reported. A number of very different interventions have been called debriefings, and the extent and the timing of these interventions vary considerably. In addition, the training and background of the debriefers are diverse, and a lack of control group or a self-selection procedure to intervention and control groups confounds accurate interpretation of results. Impressively, however, it seems that when multi-component traumatic stress strategies (e.g., CISM) that include carefully conducted CISDs as one of several interventions are used, the results are consistently positive.

I believe that the major objections against debriefings for individuals or groups are based upon the fear that a process is triggered in the survivor whereby that individual begins to seek meaningful explanations for symptoms in terms of their descriptions by the debriefer. This "sensitizing effect" occurs. It is also a fact that negative moods are more contagious than positive moods are. However, skilled group leadership will guard against such corrupting influences. It is also extremely important to ensure that psycho-educational information does not convey the sense that it is necessary to experience certain types of symptoms for the reaction to be normal.

Whatever one's opinion of debriefing, there is a moral obligation to help following critical events. I agree fully with Shalev (2000) who writes, "Debriefing has been accepted as a standard to meet obligations by many of the institutions that expose their members to stressful events, and this should not be overlooked. So far, no viable alternative has been shown to fare better (p.18), and Ursano et al. (2000) states that "Debriefing, like sleep medication or pain medication, may have little or no impact on standard health measures but still be an important intervention to limit pain, discomfort and disability" (p. 40). However, as Wilson & Sigman (2000) have pointed out, it is important to learn more about what types of debriefings are useful, for what types of persons, under what situations, and at what point in time.

When we attempt to evaluate debriefing we need to broaden our scope from simple symptom-counting to the acquisition of new coping skills, broadened and more positive perspectives on life, changes in infused or situational meaning, group cohesion and support, belief in the future, and functionality. In addition, other "objective" outcome variables such as sick leave, turnover, alcohol use, and so forth should be measured. The perspective of the consumer, or debriefing participants, who universally seem to hold these procedures in high regard, should also be kept in mind when interventions are planned in the future. Debriefing has become a very important way of caring for people where collective group cohesion and support are made available.

Individual "Debriefings"

The most often cited studies that have been used to criticize the use of debriefings have been based on a single intervention with individual medical patients (Bisson, et al., 1997; Hobbs, Mayou, Harrison & Worlock, 1996; Lee, Slade and Lygo, 1996), and not the group intervention that debriefing was originally intended to be. In addition, the debriefings have been short, usually not more than an hour (in the Bisson, et al., study the mean time was 44 minutes). In one study, Carlier, Voerman, and Gersons (2000) report an average length of 41.4 minutes for their individual debriefing with a range of 5 to 120 minutes. I wonder how it is possible to go through the different phases in five minutes. After being criticized for only having one intervention meeting, they have added follow-up debriefings. However, their second and third debriefings, what I have called follow-up debriefings, lasted an average of 17.4 and 15.9 minutes. It is a riddle how they expect to do sound clinical work with such a minimum of time. If good interventions are to be done, my experience is that you have to allow adequate time to establish rapport and then have sufficient quality time to talk about the different domains of the individual's experience. It is seldom that any debriefing takes less than two hours, as we would not use a debriefing for situations that can be so quickly handled (i.e., situations of less intensity).

This book is not about crisis intervention with individuals. I will, however, write a few words about helping individuals using the structure of the debriefing model. It is important to emphasize that the model cannot be rigorously administered. When individuals are receiving help during a crisis, it is not possible to apply the group psychological debriefing structure without adjusting the process. There is no group to normalize reactions, and this demands that the crisis intervener needs to have both the knowledge and experience to provide adequate normalization throughout and at the end of the session. Intervention with individuals assumes a different style and form, where the same areas being covered in psychological debriefing are processed (facts, thoughts, impressions, and reactions). However, normalization of reactions depends upon the facilitator's experience, and there is more freedom to go back and forth between "phases" talking about the thoughts, impressions, and reactions related to the event as the facts are outlined. This usually demands longer than a 45-minute to one-hour session, which is something that is lacking in the studies reported to date.

3

Practical Considerations When Conducting Group Psychological Debriefings

What Kind of Group Should Be Debriefed?

The selection of debriefing leaders, the organization of the meeting, and the motivation for the meeting are determined by the type of group to be debriefed. Broadly speaking, a distinction should be made between groups of people who have been exposed to a critical event as part of their work role within emergency services, police, healthcare, and primary victim groups who have survived an accident, experienced the loss of a colleague, and so forth. Usually there is more mental preparedness in the former groups. However, people in primary victim groups, such as bank or postal robbery victims, can be trained and mentally prepared as well. Mental preparedness is naturally more highly-developed in individuals who work in organizations with clear and well-defined procedures and increased awareness of the consequences of critical events, than in groups of victims exposed to a sudden event that arrived without any forewarning.

An even more important distinction is between groups of people with pre-existing social bonds, and groups of strangers that just happen to be together when they experience the critical event. People that become part of a transportation disaster will usually not be in a defined social relationship to each other. In such groups there is limited opportunity to utilize social cohesion. A "good climate" has to be established at the very outset. In groups

21

composed of strangers, the desirability of stimulating social cohesion and the development of a new social group flung together by adversity need to be carefully assessed, as this new social "connectedness" can replace and conflict with ordinary social networks. In a work-group or group of friends that experiences a critical event, the existing group climate can be of great importance for the meeting. This can either have a positive or a negative influence. For example, if already existing conflicts come to the forefront, then the effect can be very damaging to the debriefing process. On the other hand, a good pre-existing social climate predictably facilitates the debriefing process. At the outset, a group of "strangers" represents a greater challenge to the debriefing leaders because the group is more heterogeneous and there is less advance knowledge of its members. Therefore, it is recommended that such groups be led by more experienced leaders.

In the case of pre-existing groups, such as a work group, it is very advisable to gather as much information as possible about the group before the meeting goes ahead. This includes differences in work-culture. Since different occupational groups such as the police, firefighters, the military, and others, all have distinct cultures, this places considerable demands on leaders if the debriefings are to be successful. Often, cultural differences are subtle which only serves to highlight the skill involved to become a good leader.

In groups of friends or colleagues it is possible to build on existing ties of friendship and comradeship and to help the group harvest the knowledge they gain during the debriefing meetings. In such groups, the aim is to build a sense of community and cohesion to new heights. This may have consequences for the composition of the group. For example, making sure that natural members of the group in question who were not present during the critical incident are actually present during the debriefing meeting to prevent social isolation is unquestionably desirable. Likewise, larger than usual group size to accommodate everyone who should be present helps to prevent group splitting. The place selected for the debriefing is also worthy of careful thought because it should be held at a location familiar to the group that is also deemed to be safe and secure.

Role Clarification

It is recommended that two leaders conduct crisis intervention groups. There are several reasons for such a recommendation. First of all, there are so many things to be aware of and manage that it can easily become difficult for one leader. Secondly, if anyone in the group should need extra attention, e.g., leave the meeting or experience a severe emotional reaction, the co-leader can respond. Thirdly, to learn from the experience and to have a chance to discuss the process after the meeting, the second person is essential. One group leader is in charge, while the other (co-leader) assists. It is important to keep in mind, however, that the co-leader does not compete with or challenge the leader, as this very easily creates a negative climate in the whole group. If there is any sense of competition for leadership, the group will automatically sense this and it will hamper the group process. The two group leaders should know each other before meeting the group, clarify their roles before starting, and spend some time after the group to discuss how they experienced the meeting.

The way that the leader and co-leader interact during the introductory phase acts as a role model for the rest of the group. Leader and co-leader cooperation can be facilitated by the way they address each other. The use of non-verbal signals such as when the leader turns towards and lightly touches the co-leader when giving the word to him or her during the introduction shows a gentle, respectful interaction that stimulates a trustful climate that spreads to the group members.

Usually one leader is in charge of the introduction and is supported by the co-leader. The main leader goes around the group asking each participant about their experiences, while the co-leader keeps track of the group. As the group meeting evolves, the co-leader will be more active but remains supportive of the leader. The way the two leaders interact will influence the group powerfully, and can stimulate positive or create negative effects among the participants (Galinsky & Schopler, 1980). Disagreement between the leaders can instantly have a deleterious effect on the group. Effective co-leadership requires a good "chemistry" between the leaders, that their roles are clearly delineated, and that they come well-prepared [see Galinsky & Schopler (1980) for advice on co-leadership]. The group members subconsciously pick up even the way the leader looks at the co-leader during the introduction and if this is without respect and warmth, it can reduce the favorable climate of the group.

A question that is often asked is why it is not possible for two leaders to share the leadership and alternate as the meeting proceeds. This is possible and may be the easiest style to adopt from the leaders' perspective, but, with limited time, it is much easier for the participants to relate to one leader instead of two. This is especially so during the first phases of the debriefing, as they only have one person on whom to concentrate their attention. During the fact phase (to be described in more detail later), they tell "their" story to the leader and this reduces the uncertainty of whom to address. In training sessions, people sometimes want to practice shared leadership and almost invariably the feedback from the participants is that it was more confusing than having one clear leader to address comments to. The success of a debriefing does not rely on this, but it is one of the factors that augment the uninterrupted flow of the process.

Another role issue that it is important to take into account is whether or not it is possible to debrief one's own colleagues. When using peer debriefers (individuals trained in disciplines other than mental health) who are members of the group to be debriefed, this issue can become problematic. If the peer has not been properly selected, or if participants feel unsure as to whether they can talk openly about sensitive issues, the group process will be hindered. Examples include mental health professionals and trained managers. For example, if a social worker who works at an intensive care unit is planning to debrief colleagues following a critical event, it may be difficult to be totally candid because of the close working relationship. Colleagues, however professional, find it difficult to "change hats." Projections or fantasies may be transferred from the usual role into the role as a debriefer. For this reason **it is recommended that debriefers refrain from attempting to fill double roles (dual relationships).** In the example used, it would be relatively simple for the intensive care unit to use a social worker from the neighboring ward and extend their social worker to the other ward if the need arises. Of course, when peers are used as co-leaders, they should not be part of the same work team as the one to be debriefed and, if possible, not be in any chain of command that may make participants wary of what they want to disclose during the meeting.

Preparation Before the Debriefing

Although this book outlines the structure and process of group debriefings, it is important for group leaders to prepare properly, knowing exactly what they want to say during the introduction to motivate and get the group started. Besides knowing the co-leader, it can be important to establish a sign language between the leader and the co-leader so that the leader knows when the co-leader has important information or questions to contribute.

Know as much as possible about the situation to be debriefed before commencing the meeting. Digesting preliminary written reports, videotapes, newspaper clippings, and other media material is a wise preparatory move. This reduces the chance of surprises as the process unfolds. When debriefing a helping group, debriefing leaders should obtain as much information as possible about the tasks and role functions performed by the group participants as this allows them to plan for appropriate subjects or themes for discussion during the meeting. Talking to officers, commanders, supervisors, police, and others facilitates mental preparation for the task ahead. Knowledge about the critical situation makes it easier to steer the process.

When dealing with a work group, it is essential to have a clear mandate, meaning that someone within management of the organization has sanctioned the use of debriefing. Not only should it be sanctioned by the management, but also there should be clear and stated support from the management of the organization. This factor was echoed by Larsson and co-workers (1999), when they studied the conditions that affect the quality of debriefing.

Information About the Meeting

When inviting people to participate in the meetings, it is important that it is done without using psychiatric terminology or jargon that gives the impression that people are in need of therapy, or that participants must be sick or have medical problems to attend such meetings. One way of doing this is to state the following: "This is a meeting organized to talk in a structured manner about what you experienced yesterday to help you gain a better understanding on what happened, to allow the event to be put in perspective, and to provide you with information that can help you handle the experience, so that it does not bother you over time."

When participants are being invited or motivated to attend a debriefing meeting, the leader should discuss with the organizer how the meeting will be introduced to the potential participants. Often it is advisable to ask, "How will you phrase the invitation to the meeting?" The purpose of this is to find a good way of presenting what the process is about, clear up possible misunderstandings, and help the organizer motivate the group for participation.

Place

The debriefing should be held in an environment free of distractions, preferably in a room that has windows but which allows privacy, is well-ventilated, and is well-lit. Its size should be appropriate for the number of participants, with tables and comfortable chairs which can be adapted to the size of the group. People with mobile phones should be asked to turn them off, and the room for the meeting should be as quiet as possible. A sign on the door can notify people where the meeting is taking place and should state "Please Do Not Disturb" to reduce interruptions from outside. Remember that if the situation demands, debriefings can be held in less than ideal locations.

Timing

There is no absolute "best" time to conduct a debriefing, although care should be taken not to take a group through all the phases of the debriefing process too close to the event. The reasons for this differ depending upon the group to be debriefed. For personnel involved in disaster work that continues over several days or weeks, systematic talk-throughs should be postponed until their duties are finished. While their work is ongoing, emergency personnel usually employ different coping strategies to be able to concentrate on their tasks and keep any emotional reactions at bay while doing their work. To be able to do so, they seldom can get in touch with the emotional ramifications of an event if the debriefing takes place too soon after the event. A defusing, which allow the workers a chance to talk about whatever they give priority, will be welcome at this point. However, new research where robbery victims were randomly allocated to immediate (<10 hours) or delayed (>48 hours) CISDs found those who received the immediate debriefing developed fewer and less severe posttraumatic stress symptoms on each of four times for measurement in the first two weeks after the event (Campfield & Hills, 2001). Whether this evidence in support of early debriefing will generalize to other traumatic events and populations remains to be studied. The study by Campfield & Hills (2001) points to the need for an increased understanding on timing issues regarding early intervention.

The primary focus of immediate interventions, whether for individuals, families, or groups, are to: a) provide comfort and care, and to reduce arousal (creating a caring climate), and b) secure information for those affected. Immediately after a trauma, people are in a situation where their senses are sharpened to allow rapid intake of information. Although much debated, new memory research suggests that in situations of intense arousal, memory enhancement mechanisms are activated (van der Kolk & Fisler, 1995). This is a phenomenon I have tentatively called "supermemory" (Dyregrov, 1992) to emphasize the intense, vivid memory that can be experienced following such situations. At the same time, many individuals experience reduced emotional reactivity (or dissociation), as well as memory loss (Joseph, 1999). I believe this sharpening of the senses and dissociation are part of a mobilization of mental resources that help us cope with a critical event. It secures intake of information which, together with focused attention on important aspects of the situation, rapid utilization of previous experience, and learning stored in memory, allow people to respond appropriately (see Dyregrov, Solomon & Bassøe, 2000). The sharpening of the senses also means that the caring climate has the potential to be felt as very caring and helpful or distant, cold and unhelpful. This makes it extremely important that a well-structured and well-thought-out system is organized for immediate intervention.

For ordinary people experiencing a critical event, there are sound reasons for delaying formal debriefing beyond the 24 hours. The mental mobilization that takes place (Dyregrov, Solomon & Bassøe, 2000) may lead to feelings of unreality and a post-ponement of absorption of all the ramifications of the event. The postponement of the emotional reaction allows all personal resources to be mobilized to cope with the situation. At this time it is unwise to pressure people through a systematic review of the event. If some time is allowed before the debriefing takes place, the prospect is that it will be more successful in achieving its aims because participants will have been allowed some time to establish "emotional" contact with the situation. This "protective shield" needs to be better understood for us to know when to most appropriately time both the group interventions and the early interventions for individuals.

This does not mean that there cannot be good support provided before the debriefing for both individuals and groups, in the form of providing facts about the situation, and the possibility to talk about what happened.

Sometimes several days or even weeks elapse before it is possible to sit down as a group to talk through a critical event. Although benefits of acceleration of normalization that an early debriefing provides will be lost (Robinson & Mitchell, 1993), it can still be a powerful tool in helping the group. The following case exemplifies this point:

> *Years ago I was called upon to debrief a U.N. group following a critical event in which a person was killed and another injured. Unfortunately, for a number of reasons no immediate debriefing was held. One did take place six months after the event, when the U.N. agency sought assistance. The event had resulted in several of the survivors who were in a leadership position becoming unable to perform their duties adequately. Even though the survivor group had had sufficient time to talk through what happened, it was not until the more formal debriefing took place six months later that they were able to fit the different parts of the puzzle together. In addition to the debriefing information, meetings were held for all staff. Some individuals received one-on-one help and management were advised on how to create better systems for the future. Although the debriefing was a crucial part of this intervention, it was part of a multifaceted intervention that can be classified as a CISM-intervention. It was a testament to its usefulness that the regional manager of the agency asked if further debriefings could be held in several other locations where other staff members were suffering as a result of being exposed to critical events.*

Mitchell, Schiller, Eyler, and Everly (1999) describe a similar, more comprehensive multifaceted intervention (including a CISD) initiated more than three years after a tornado tragedy. Many children were killed and this seriously affected firefighters in the small community. A majority of the firefighters had a significant reduction of posttraumatic stress symptoms following this intervention, even after years of ongoing problems.

Chemtob and co-workers (1997) used debriefing plus a two hour lecture on "post disaster recovery," carried out six and nine (delayed intervention) months following a hurricane. This showed that debriefing can be effective a long time after the time period recommended for debriefing. This is similar to what was reported by Stallard and Law (1993) in their study of adolescents who survived a mini-bus traffic accident.

Debriefing techniques have also been incorporated in a brief group psychotherapy program to treat established PTSD following a broad range of traumatic situations including combat (Busuttil & Turnbull et al., 1995). With psychological debriefing being the main therapeutic feature of a 12-day structured in-patient group psychotherapy "course" that also includes psycho-education and cognitive restructuring, and with one-day group follow-up sessions over a one-year period, the authors were able to show highly significant improvement. This study, although using debriefing techniques within a therapy framework, suggests that the use of group debriefing may also be useful in the treatment of PTSD, even when implemented long after the traumatic exposure occurred.

If a good defusing (a much shorter variant of a debriefing) has been conducted, it may be appropriate to wait longer, even a week, before the debriefing, as this allows for more specific advice concerning problems that may have developed, as well as more accumulated experience to use in the sharing of coping methods. Also, when personnel return from longer missions, for example humanitarian assistance workers, my advice is to let staff have some time at home before bringing them back to a more formal discussion of their experience. On such occasions, they will not only talk about one event, but a series of more or less critical situations or periods of extreme stress. In these situations, the usual debriefing session might have to be spread over several days, as Turnbull (1997) has advocated following hostage-takings in which hostages have been held for long periods of time. It may be unwise to force people in such situations to take part in a statutory intervention before being reunited with their families, for example, as was the case for the U.S. hostages held in Iran in the late 1970s.

In my experience and that of others (Tehrani, 1998), one should be careful in conducting group debriefings or individualized crisis intervention for persons who have suffered physical injury while they are still healing their physical wounds or experiencing pain. This does not mean that patients who want to talk about their injuries, or the situation that caused them, should not be allowed to do so. But to actively instigate or force anyone to do so does not take into account the fact that for many, the physical healing takes priority over the emotional ramifications of the event. This means that burn patients who must undergo painful procedures must be allowed to process the emotional aspects of their injury at their own pace and not automatically be taken through a detailed review of all aspects of their traumatic experience. Unfortunately, some of the studies that have found no benefits or a negative effect from individualized "debriefing" have done just that, and used a structured debriefing format shortly after a patient has been hospitalized either with a burn injury (Bisson, et al., 1997) or traffic injury (Hobbs et al., 1996).

As more research on early intervention is conducted and we gather more knowledge, we may see a time when we organize debriefings in a different manner than we do today. Shalev, Pitman, Orr, Peri, & Brandes (2000) collected data two days following combat exposure and found that dissociative symptoms significantly correlated with better evaluation of group and individual performance during combat. If debriefings are conducted in this period (the recommended timeframe), it may reduce the effectiveness of dissociation as a distancing defense. Dissociation, on the other hand, has also been related to the later development of PTSD (Spiegel, Koopman & Classen, 1994; Foa & Riggs, 1995; Marmar, Weiss, Metzler, Ronfeldt & Foreman,

1996). This represents a cogent argument in favor of using debriefing to bring about association (contact between emotional and cognitive aspects of the experience). Recently, Watchorn (2000) has found that peritraumatic dissociation (feelings of detachment during or immediately after an event) predicted long-term impairment and PTSD, but for those who dissociated, subsequent debriefings were associated with less impairment. However, if this involves an insensitive exposure to traumatic detail, it may strengthen the dissociation instead of reducing it. Only further research conducted on differently timed debriefings will tell us what point will be optimal for this group intervention. We should also bear in mind that the optimum time will probably need to take into account the kind of group that is to be debriefed, and the kind of situation the participants have dealt with or experienced.

One note of caution: when people are still involved in the performance of their duties following disasters, or continue to be in dangerous or ongoing traumatizing situations, such as being part of a U.N. emergency mission, one should be careful about the timing of debriefings. This may render their defenses less useful. With ongoing disaster situations there must be ongoing measures to secure their health during the mission, perhaps with some form of closure meeting at the end of a day's work, in order to ease the transition and demobilization. The following case demonstrates that point:

> *During a U.N. emergency operation, the leader introduced a section at the end of regular staff meetings during the week where a short review of how people were doing was conducted. In addition to taking "the pulse" of the group, other stress reducing measures were introduced (such as more leisure activities or rest and recovery leaves). The leaders of different sections of the U.N. group conducted similar reviews among their staff as well. In addition, the leader who was accustomed to keeping very long working hours (first to arrive early morning and last to leave late at night)*

was advised on the signs that this sent out to the rest of the staff, who felt guilty if they attended to their own needs. By becoming more aware of the example he created for others, he managed to change this pattern and also attend to his own exhaustion.

Group Size

It is hard for people to talk in large groups. **For this reason the group size should be a maximum of 15 people. I find a group size between 8 to 12 people to be ideal.** The experience within a very small group (< 5) becomes less varied, and smaller groups do not allow for the same normalization by hearing that others reacted in similar ways. In some situations, larger groups need to be conducted because of the high number of people that have to be debriefed or the lack of trained debriefing leaders. Sometimes a very cohesive group makes it inadvisable to break the group down into smaller groups. If possible, the group size should be less than 15 people, as larger groups often become less helpful for the participants.

Group Composition

The issue of group composition can be very challenging. Who should be in the group? Should it be divided according to degrees of exposure to the incident, gender, or authority? Should the group be heterogeneous or homogeneous? There are no "absolute" answers to this, and it will be the particular circumstances which define or determine the composition of the group. As a general rule, it is important to try to prevent those who have been highly exposed in a sensory way (those who have witnessed, heard, smelled, or touched) from relating detailed versions of their experience to those relatively unexposed. Later in the book I will explain this in more detail, but **suffice it to say that one should guard against traumatizing people by exposing them to detailed reports of a traumatic incident that they will not be able to use constructively.**

My experience has been that **homogeneous groups are the**

most desirable. This can be illustrated by the following: if survivors from a train disaster are simply divided into different groups without attention to which carriage they sat in, the chances are that they will only meet some of the people who may hold important facts regarding their survival. If, however, the groups are divided according to the carriage they actually sat in, those in physical proximity to each other can "fill in the blanks" and get a total picture of what happened to them as they left the carnage.

In 1986, Thoits discussed social support as a form of coping assistance and pointed out the following: **"Practically speaking, coping aid from others who have faced or who currently face similar stressors and who have experienced similar reactions should be highly efficacious."** "Conversely, dissimilarity in social background and life experience (and thus lower empathy) should result in ineffective, if not damaging, attempts at coping aid" (p. 421).

There can also be good reasons to organize more heterogeneous groups, as they may provide a broader variety of coping skills, experience, and perspective. However, participants usually gain most benefit from sharing the time with those who have the most parallel experiences.

With regard to groups involving work colleagues, it is important to note who is present or absent during the debriefing:

> *A bank was robbed twice within a year. Psychological debriefings were conducted following both robberies. I did not conduct the debriefings, but met with staff as part of a follow-up meeting. One of the employees started to cry during the meeting. Afterwards she explained that she had not been present during these two armed robberies. The first occurred some days before she started working in the bank; the other took place when she was at home with a sick child. She complained that she felt excluded from the group, as they had become a very cohesive group, supportive of each other, but with "little room" for others.*

Based on this and other examples of group-exclusion

mechanisms that I have observed following debriefings, **I have included members of natural work groups not present during the critical events in the meetings.** Not only does this reduce the risk of group exclusion, but also those not present during the event will better understand what their colleagues have experienced and social support may more easily be solicited. The inclusion of people not present during a critical event is most important when one or a few of a cohesive work group were absent. It is, however, not beneficial to have too many participants who were not involved.

Another difficult group composition issue is whether or not to have people in leadership positions, e.g., managers or supervisors, present during the debriefing. If they took part in the event, they naturally belong in the meeting. If they were involved in the planning or operational aspects or were distanced from the event, they may also be included. However, if they were away at the time or were not part of the incident, there may be good reason not to have them present, as some participants may be reluctant to say things in fear that this will have some negative consequence for them in the future. Although the manager or senior person may not see this as a problem and emphasizes his/her good relationship with the staff, there may still be subtle processes that will inhibit others if they are present. Some authors suggest separate groups for workers and managers (Armstrong, Lund, McWright, & Tichenor, 1995). As will be described later, if conflicts are present before the event, the use of a debriefing group may not be advisable and group composition must receive careful attention.

Sometimes children are part of the affected group. **The question whether to include children in the debriefing meeting becomes an issue. There are no easy answers to this question.** For example, if there was a bus collision where a few children were survivors together with an adult, I would suggest that children are included to ensure that they get access to the same facts as adults. However, this demands that the leaders who run the debriefing have experience in dealing with children's responses to trauma. Older children (>10 years of age) can be part of the whole debriefing, while younger children may benefit from the fact phase and then can meet directly with a mental health professional to continue the process. If several children survived or were deeply affected by a traumatic event, my suggestion would be to run a special debriefing group for children. If one is meeting with an extended family to conduct a debriefing, my suggestion will again be to include the children (Dyregrov, 1997a).

Regardless of group composition, **it is advisable that the participants are motivated ahead of the meeting in such a way that they come with the attitude that it is a good investment.** This is best achieved by having a leader within the organization who has credibility and a good reputation explain what the debriefing process is about and advocate for their attendance of the group. This may mean that one of the debriefing leaders spends some time on providing input or help on what he/she can tell the group. Following some Norwegian disasters, we have been so successful in this respect that we have had individual emergency workers turning up directly after being discharged from the disaster area demanding to be debriefed because their leader had talked so favorable about this opportunity. Following large-scale events, written information that explains the purpose of debriefings to encourage participation will have to be provided.

Seating Positions

The group may be seated in a circle, having one group leader sit at one side of the circle and another opposite them. Another choice is to sit around a rectangular table with the group leaders sitting at the top of the table with the participants evenly spread around the table. The latter choice is usually better. The table should not be too wide as this creates distance within the group and there should be no empty chairs around the table, as this also will impair the group process. I favor the second seating position as it emphasizes the clear leadership and the physical proximity of the two leaders and allows for easier communication between the two. Although visual contact is easier when sitting opposite each other in a circular group, when sitting beside each other one can easily exchange a few words and use non-verbal signals to indicate one's wish to say something as a co-leader. Smooth and respectful interaction between the leaders is also easy to note for the participants and positively influences the climate in the group.

The rectangular seating position allows the leaders to have an overview of the whole group, as long as the tables are not too narrow. However, it is sometimes difficult for the group participants on one side of the table to see those talking on the same side of the table. A circular seating configuration is more democratic as all participants have the same opportunity to see each other. As a leader, however, it may be difficult to pick up the cues from the individuals seated nearest to you on each side. For the same reason it is important not to have anyone seated too far up on either side of the table as they easily slip out of one's vision.

Seating positions may also be chosen depending upon the culture of the group. In many countries, health personnel, such as nurses, have a tradition for sitting in a circular group when having their daily handover meetings. When that is the case, one needs to conform to this familiar seating position, as it will be the position least likely to increase anxiety. The culture of one's country will also determine what physical set-up one will use. In the U.S., the circular position is more used than in Scandinavia. For an older generation, this way of sitting invokes the image of Jack Nicholson in a psychiatric therapy group in *One Flew Over the Cuckoo's Nest*. Such an association may easily raise their anxiety level and make the start of the process harder. My choice of having a table in front of the participant is quite deliberate, as it provides more structure and security than sitting "undressed" without a table in front. Most people are accustomed to having a table in front of them during a meeting, and this familiar position makes the participants feel more secure at the outset when uncertainty is usually at a maximum. Younger people seldom have the same idea and we often use the circular set-up in debriefings for adolescents.

Other Practical Matters

Beverages should be present in the room before starting, but coffee should be avoided as this leads to increased arousal. If food is to be served, it should also be present before the meeting so that people can help themselves during the meeting without interrupting the process. Such nourishment may also be provided after the meeting to avoid disturbing the process unnecessarily. **The time of day often determines what refreshments to provide.** If the meeting is destined to last through lunch it is better if stomach cramps do not divert attention away from the content of the meeting.

4

The Phases of Psychological Debriefing

The Structure

My own experience, as well the experience of others, over time and within different cultures have demonstrated that the debriefing structure outlined below has proven to be effective. Flexibility is also always needed when conducting debriefings. Sometimes the structure has to be abandoned because the needs of the group demand it. Those with little experience should stick to the model as closely as possible and deviate from it only as they gain more experience as leaders.

The structure of the meeting is as follows[1] :

- **Introduction**
    — introduction of leaders
    — rules
    — purpose of meeting
    — overview of meeting
- **Facts**
    — concrete experiences of participants
    — go around the group

---

[1] In Appendix A a short form or a memory aid for the structure of the meeting can be found. This can be printed on a card and brought to the meeting.

- **Thoughts**
  - early thoughts, later thoughts
  - important decisions
  - mental mobilization or constructive thoughts
- **Sensory impressions**
  - carefully review when appropriate
- **Reactions**
  - questions about thoughts often lead to emotional answers
  - what was the worst about what happened
  - immediate reactions, later and current reactions (emotional, behavioral, somatic)
- **Normalization**
  - comment on similarity in experiences and reactions
  - provide information about expected reactions
  - advise on coping strategies
  - provide written material
- **Future planning and closure**
  - summarize learning
  - plan additional follow-up meetings if needed

Most debriefing meetings will follow this structure, although the phases sometimes mingle, and sometimes parts may have to be more superficially discussed. In the different phases, the leader emphasizes different aspects to achieve different aims.

Arriving at the Debriefing Venue

I advise arrival at the place where the debriefing is to be undertaken well ahead of time. This leaves time for organizing the room in the best possible way to facilitate the process, but most importantly, it provides an opportunity to meet informally with participants as they arrive. This has a dual purpose. The first is to let the participants have a chance to familiarize themselves with you as well as to reduce any anticipatory anxiety they might have regarding "debriefers." The second is that leaders get a golden opportunity to assess the participants and to note their style of interaction and communication. If some people appear to be very nervous then it may be possible to reduce tension, to offer some reassuring words, and to notice anyone with particular needs. Team members should split up and circulate before settling down and may ask simple questions to get a better grasp of the task at hand. It might be pertinent for the leaders to ask if the group has been involved in a similar situation before.

The different phases of the debriefing are outlined in more detail in the following table:

Leader Activity	Aim
Introduction Introduce leaders, purpose, and rules for the debriefing.	Establish favorable climate decrease anxiety, and build trust. Signal structure.
Fact Phase Help relate facts and review event.	Create wholeness and joint understanding. Fill in blanks. In vitro exposure.
Thought Phase Help relate thoughts and decisions.	Stimulate coherent understanding. Help understand the background for decisions made and actions taken.
Sensory Impression Phase Stimulate a detailed review of sensory images. Give words to sensory images. Not applicable to all debriefings.	Prevent later intrusive images. Make implicit memories explicit. Reduce arousal.
Reaction Phase Help participants to relate emotional and somatic reactions to event.	Decrease emotional involvement and identification with the situation. Gain perspective.

Table continued on next page

Psychological Debriefing

Leader Activity	Aim
Stimulate confrontation and exposure in vitro.	Secure more rapid normalization.
If work-group: discuss role-related problems.	Prevent avoidance behavior. Ventilation. Plan for clearer role definitions and better interaction.
Activate group or team resources through the group process: 1) sharing of responsibility 2) normalization 3) sharing of coping strategies.	Mobilize group or team support. Prevent rumination and blame. Enhance coping resources.
Normalization Phase Provide verbal and written information.	More rapid normalization. Provide frame of reference.

Suggest coping strategies and concrete suggestions on how to handle common problems:
1) handling intrusive images
2) relaxation, self-talk
3) write about the event
4) stress management advice
  i.e., regulate intake of
  coffee, sugar; exercise
	More control over intrusive material. Help to structure event by themselves. Decrease of arousal and fear activated processes. Counteracting avoidance.

Future Planning and Closure Focus on lessons learned, i.e., acquisition of new coping skills and perception of growth. Information about follow-up resources. Personal contact for those who want it. Arrangement for follow-up debriefing, if needed.	Secure future coping. Acknowledge positive factors. Have access to further help.

The Introduction Phase

Introduction of the Leaders

The **most important phase of the debriefing is the introduction**. It is designed to:

- Provide structure
- Define boundaries
- Build trust
- Decrease anxiety and foster acceptance
- Establish temporary or lasting cohesiveness
- Motivate participants
- Prepare for phases to come.

This is when the participants gear up their motivation to invest in the meeting and also when they develop trust in the leaders that is necessary for open communication. The way that the group leaders introduce and present themselves is crucially important. Group leaders need to "sell" themselves to establish trust. Participants need to be able to sense that the group leaders have the necessary authority and knowledge to handle the meeting. During the introduction, the group leader initially describes his/ her background without the use of sophisticated phrases. This presentation should not consist of only one sentence, but should include a description of the background and experience that he/ she has for leading such meetings. After the leader has completed the introduction, the co-leader should do the same.

The leader's task is to establish an atmosphere of trust in the group, quickly outline the goals, and motivate for participation. In the first part of the debriefing, he/she builds a relationship with the group and its individual members. Sensitive methods of asking questions and attentive, respectful, and interested attitudes permit the leader to become a role model for the group. The leader also has to select the agenda and allocate time for important issues that emerge during the meeting, as well as to guard against destructive group processes. By their directness, honesty, respect, encouragement, enthusiasm, and vitality, the group leaders can activate and model responses for individual participants and the whole group.

Purpose of the Meeting

Following the introduction, the group leader should say why it is important to have such meetings and emphasize how this will help people organize their experience and add structure and cohesion to what happened. Aims are described as including:

· Understanding how and why an event happened
· Having a chance to put words to all aspects of an event and putting them in order of sequence
· Understanding why reactions occur in a certain way, i.e., explaining the event to oneself
· Learning that others often react in a similar way as oneself
· Having a chance to get information about common reactions and how to handle them.

New facts and different perspectives often emerge, and this helps participants to get a more complete picture of what happened and to fill in any blanks. In addition, it should be emphasized that there is also an opportunity to get advice to improve coping strategies for the future. Experience has shown that those who talk about traumatic events resume their normal lives faster. If the group to be debriefed is a work group, it may improve morale and develop more constructive ways of handling future critical events. Good leadership will engender confidence in the participants and stimulate motivation to follow through the entire debriefing process.

Rules

Rules are important steering tools for the group process and will help prevent negative group experiences. They include:

· Confidentiality
· Voluntary active participation
· Participants being encouraged to talk about their own impressions and reactions, and not what they have heard from others

- Democratic use of the group's time
- Respect for other participants
- No note taking, tape recordings, etc.

Rules are introduced in the following manner: "From experience we know that it is important to have some guidelines for meetings such as this. First of all, it is important that people can talk in here without fearing that others will repeat personal information that they hear outside the group. I therefore want an agreement that the things said in here will be kept in here (get acknowledgement from group). Of course there are no limits to what you can tell about your own thoughts and reactions to others outside this meeting, but what you hear other people say about their thoughts, impressions, and reactions should not be repeated outside this room." This is the only rule that may be important to repeat at the end of the meeting so that people don't leave the meeting afraid that others will learn things that they do not want them to know.

The other rules can be presented in the same straightforward manner. It is important to tell them that although they are not required to say anything, except from giving an outline of what they experienced (fact phase), they would make the best use of the meeting if they contribute to the discussion. However, when somebody chooses to listen and not to say much, it is his/her choice and it should be respected. The rule about democratic use of the group's time is to limit those who may dominate the discussion. However, when drawing the attention of a group member to this rule, it is important to be friendly and impersonal. If the same person has to be reminded several times, then firmness of the intervention needs to be increased and the member reminded that all participants in the group must get a chance to contribute equally.

In some groups, other rules have to be added. For example, in helper groups one may state that: "This is not a technical or tactical debriefing, this is a meeting organized to have a chance to talk about thoughts and reactions that resulted from the event."

In other groups it is important to make sure that no outsiders are present, for example, members of the press, or people who are present just to learn from the other participants. Following a transportation disaster when participants have been invited to participate by using media resources, it may be advisable to ask: "Is there anyone present that was not on board the train the day before yesterday?" In this way one can make sure that the group is composed only of the participants it was actually planned for and that "observers" do not slow the process down or cause it to fail. However, in a work group, it may be important to include someone who was absent on the day the critical event happened to maintain their inclusion as part of the group and thus not feel isolated from the others.

Overview Of The Meeting

At the end of the introduction phase, the leader provides an outline of the whole meeting by saying, for example: "What will happen now is that we first go around the group and each person will get a chance to give a brief outline on what they have experienced. After going around the group, we will address some of the thoughts you had during the experience and some other thoughts you are left with afterwards. Next, we will focus on some of the sensory impressions you have faced during this event, before we use time on the reactions you have experienced. Following this, we would like to give you some information on common reactions to critical incidents and some advice on what you can do to help yourself or your family. At the end of the meeting we will discuss whether we should meet again. It is hard to say exactly how long this meeting will take, but we expect it to take a couple of hours."

If, during the introduction, the leader gives too much eye contact and attention to one side of the group, or if he/she looks at only one person, or even worse, gives little eye contact by focusing on a spot at the back of the room, parts of, or the whole group will feel overlooked. During video-based training, I have learned that such non-verbal cues of attention are crucial in setting the climate for the rest of the debriefing. During the introduction, the debriefing leader should let his/her eyes and head move from one side of the group to the other, giving eye contact to all the participants. Body posture is also important, as it signals attention and respect to the group. In western cultures, this means leaning the upper body towards the group showing an engaged body posture. Members will unconsciously recognize this, and it will encourage the involvement of participants and a sense of respect. This may seem obvious to experienced group leaders, but during the training of debriefers, few have seemed to be intuitively aware of how they address a group.

Words To Use During The Introduction

People who attend a debriefing following a critical situation will, as a result of the mobilization of mental processes, be vigilant about what is happening around them, as this reaction has an intrinsic survival value. Having such "sharpened senses" makes them very sensitive to verbal and non-verbal cues, including sensitivity to how the debriefing leader uses and phrases his/her words. If the leader talks about how "terrible this has been for all of us" and includes him/herself as having been affected by the event, the participants may say to themselves "Have we come here for his/her sake or for us?" Or, "What does he/she know, he/she was not there." Also, if the leader talks about "I can understand how this must be for you" or uses similar phraseology, the participants may decide to ignore the process because they know that he/she cannot possibly appreciate fully how they feel.

Some words may also scare the participants, for example, the word "feelings" or "feel": "We will talk about some of the feelings you experienced." Some will feel threatened by being expected to express their feelings. Participants like the word "reactions" better, as it appears less threatening to talk about reactions. Leaders should also be careful about using the word "psychiatry" or "psychiatric" when referring to their backgrounds, as this is not what the majority of participants associate with their situation. For example: "My experience is drawn from 14 years of work at a psychiatric hospital ...." would be better phrased as, "I have for many years worked with people who experience difficult situations." Such careful use of words avoids the impression that participants are in need of psychiatric help. Heightened sensitivity to the words the debriefers use makes it even more important to have planned well what to say and how to say it during the introduction.

The Fact Phase

During the fact-phase, each participant is encouraged to tell his/her story of what they have experienced. To be remembered in the fact phase is the following:

- Be precise in what you want participants to tell you during this phase.
- Start going around the group by following the normal culture for meetings (left to right), or start by the order the participants became involved in the event.
- Use the group to help participants build up a complete "picture" of what happened.
- Let the group members provide information if someone has memory gaps.
- Facilitate relationship-building by follow-up questions.
- Seek out further facts at the end of the fact phase (from the whole group) if something is unclear or left out.

It is important for the group leader to be precise in what he/she wants the participants to tell during this phase. With an open invitation such as "tell me what you experienced," participants may start to talk about emotions and reactions and the debriefing-leader easily loses control. Some group members may experience an over-rapid progression into emotions as frightening and it may cause them to be cautious and hold back later. When starting the fact phase it is best to be specific, for example, in the following way: "I would first like you to tell about how you learned about what happened the day before yesterday and your involvement (role) in what took place (tailor the question to the event) and what happened from your point of view. Later we will get back to some of the thoughts and reactions you had, but at this time please give a brief account of what happened from your perspective." As you say this, use your eyes to indicate where you are going to start by looking at that person a couple of times. Then they are prepared and feel forewarned. Start by going around the group following the normal culture for this, usually from left to right in the group, or start with the first one who got involved. In some situations, one person has been under severe exposure during the critical event, for example, having a knife to his/her throat. In such cases, it is imperative to talk to the person before the debriefing starts and ask whether she wants to start or would prefer to speak later.

If the group consists of ten or more people, it is important to avoid lengthy descriptions otherwise there will be insufficient time left for the other parts of the debriefing. However, my experience from trainings commonly demonstrates that leaders spend too little time on the facts. Following an event that is redolent with factual information, at least three to four minutes spent on each person will usually be needed to get a thorough description of what happened. Remember that something such as a suicide by a colleague that happened with none of the work group present is a low fact situation. With small groups (<5) it is easier to let each person have even more time to give detail to their experiences.

When moving around the group, the group leader will establish a relationship with each individual member. This is done by being very attentive to what each participant is saying and by non-verbal acknowledgement. For example, nodding or moving closer to the person when something very important is declared and by giving total attention and listening hard to what the person says can accomplish this.

The co-leader is able to notice when certain themes assume importance for other members of the group and store this for later use during the reaction phase. A relationship with each participant is established, as each participant is provided time for telling their story. This relationship has three elements. First, it is facilitated by giving the person clear indications that it is his or her turn, i.e., by looking directly at this person, stretching out the arm with the palm towards him/her and then saying something like "Maybe you can continue...." Secondly, the relationship is further established by asking follow-up questions regarding the facts described. During this interaction, the debriefing leader gives full attention to the person talking. The last element of this relationship building is the ending, where the debriefing leader acknowledges the response. A smile, nod, and a thank-you (or similar expression) achieves this well. This last part is often forgotten and group leaders just move their eyes to the next participant without acknowledging the story they have received.

This careful way of building a relationship with each and every member creates a climate that is good for sharing personal information and it builds trust in the leader. If something is unclear regarding the facts, I advise asking at this point. If some facts are unclear for the member who is speaking, other members of the group might have additional facts that can clarify what happened for the person.

Following a train crash, a mother was knocked unconscious and did not know what her pre-school daughter had seen or heard. It was a year later, and all too late that a "debriefing" was held. At that time, other survivors of the crash were able to inform her about some of the things that took place when she was unconscious. For her, this meant she could answer some of the questions her daughter had asked her.

The Thought Phase

Some of the important aspects of the thought phase are:
- To follow time sequence (early and then later thoughts)
- To focus on decisions and activity
- To seek out elements reflecting mental mobilization

- To notice obvious and hidden feeling themes revealed by thoughts
- To enquire about some of the "unstated" thoughts?

After each participant has had a chance to tell their story, the debriefing-leader should briefly start the next phase by saying something like this: "What were some of the first thoughts you had (or thoughts that went through your mind) when this happened?" This question is addressed to the whole group and whoever wants to start will start. Please remember that it may take some time before participants access their thoughts. Start with early thoughts, and then proceed to thoughts that came later during their experiences. If the group to be debriefed is an emergency responder group, I advise asking: "What were some of the thoughts that went through your head as you were going to the scene?" This will provide insight in how prepared the emergency workers were for the situation they had to deal with. Sometimes the lack of mental preparation can explain reactions experienced at the scene, or one can point out how well they coped because they had made a plan on how to deal with the situation.

Years ago following a bus crash that killed 14 children and two adults, rescuers who were asked about their thoughts on responding to the event (driving time to this fairly remote place was as long as 45 to 60 minutes for some responding units) stated that among their thoughts were: "What if the passengers on the bus are Italians? I do not know a word of Italian." Many others had similar thoughts, and through their first thoughts we learned that very few (only those who came late) knew that there were children involved, and most came mentally unprepared for this. The first notice of the disaster did not include any information about this being a bus full of children.

Asking about the thoughts that emergency workers have when responding to an event provides good information on mental preparation, as well as the team perception of the event.

Often, when people struggle with problems following critical or traumatic events or losses, it is because they are blaming themselves for their own responses or lack of such, or they may view their thoughts and behavior as inappropriate. By specifically asking for the thoughts that went through a person's head when they made important decisions or experienced their traumas, it often becomes clear for them that although they feel helpless afterwards, they were, in fact, able to think constructively and make decisions that were important for surviving the situation. For this reason, asking about what thoughts they had during the traumatic experience helps the participants to get in contact with resources that helped them survive. In this important phase, negative thought patterns and inappropriate self-blame can be reversed, often by the active use of the group to counteract such thinking. The leader can seek out elements that reflect mental mobilization.

> *During a debriefing where a U.N. driver had saved the lives of his passengers due to his rapid response when he quickly reversed the car when they were ambushed, he was asked what were the thoughts that made him respond so appropriately. He answered that the very same morning the U.N. drivers had discussed what they were to do if they were ambushed. It was proposed that reversing the car and backing out of the situation would pose less of a threat to the passengers than trying to drive forwards and exposing the non-armoured side of the car. One person was shot and killed in the car, but by focusing on the constructive thoughts that saved the other passengers, they felt less helpless than before the debriefing.*

Mental mobilization is characterized by rapid use of stored information—a search through accumulated experience to find relevant ways for handling the situation. In addition, it consists of a sharpened sensory intake that allows for rapid decisions, focused attention on important aspects of the situation, and an altered time sense that allows for extra time to make decisions. Finally, this survival mechanism often involves a postponement of emotional reactions that help people stay focused on their survival. By seeking out and pinpointing elements that reflect such mental mobilization, I have often been able to help people understand that they were not helpless but actually took an active part in securing their own and others' survival.

During the thought phase, both leader and co-leader will notice obvious and hidden feelings revealed by the thoughts. From these they identify themes that should be addressed during the reaction phase.

The Sensory Impression Phase

Sensory stimulation during critical events often leads to the formation of strong sensory images. These impressions or images are frequently found in a fragmented form in the mind, and a detailed verbal expression can help take some of the "power" out of them, as well as bring the whole event into a coherent story. Brewin (2001) highlighted the existence of two different memory systems. One is characterized by "verbally accessible memory" or VAM. This is readily available and characterizes ordinary autobiographical memory. The other, called "situationally accessible memory" or SAM, supports the specific trauma-related dreams and re-experiencing (flashbacks) characteristic of PTSD. SAM is more concerned with perceptual processing after a trauma and also the somatic responses. SAM-type imprints are detailed and affect-laden but are also non-verbal and therefore it is more difficult to communicate their content to others or to integrate it in autobiographical memory. A strong dissociation during the trauma, as well as marked avoidance afterwards, are believed to compound the problem of understanding the content of SAM. Everything that impedes the creation of detailed, conscious memory for the most intense moments of the event will cause problems in comprehension afterwards. Brewin (2001) believes that the more aspects of the situational accessible memory can be transferred to the verbal memory, the more comprehension is possible. At the same time, he cautions against over-energetic stimulation while this process of transfer of SAM to VAM is under way, as this can actually hinder transmission of information between the two memory systems. **The sensory impression phase of the debriefing can be one way of fitting words to the sensory impressions formed in different channels, i.e., making them verbally accessible. Psychological debriefing can help convert vague emotional memory imprints into verbal analogues.**

It is important when leading this phase to:

- Let the group decide which sensory experience to start with.
- Take time on each sensory channel.
- Let the group give words to the worst aspects.
- Explore in detail different aspects of the impressions.
- Be careful when parts of the group had no sensory exposure.
- Provide individual help for participants who have experienced "graphic" impressions.

When members of the group have similar sensory impressions, they can give words to the various impressions in the group and through these transform sensory fragments into a verbal collage that is both cogent and meaningful. This technique facilitates a "collective narrative" that effectively verbalizes sensory memory. It does not matter which group participant finds appropriate words to describe the frequently complex aspects of a sensory impression because as soon as the description is heard in the group, other members benefit by having access to a verbal analogue. In some respects, this parallels poetry where poets help to put deeply felt collective wisdom into words.

There is a theoretical danger of traumatizing others if the details are too concrete and grotesque and therefore this phase should be handled with skill and care. It may be sensible to screen out those with the most compelling and noxious sensory impressions and facilitate individual help for them afterwards.

If there is homogeneity in the group exposure, the group leaders should take time on each sensory channel and help the participants give words to visual, auditory, olfactory (smell), and tactile impressions. Sometimes there are taste impressions as well. Let the group decide what sensory channel they want to describe first by asking: "What sensory impression do you remember most vividly?" If they start describing visual impressions, make sure that this channel is covered thoroughly before going on to the next. This can be done by the following questions: "What other visual impressions are imprinted at the back of your mind?" and "Other visual impressions?" By asking about different qualities of these sensory impressions (i.e., for visual images; color, form or shape, brightness, distance), the group leader will help participants to give words to these impressions. They also help reduce or prevent these impressions from returning to haunt them during day and/or night as the sensory impressions naturally seek their verbal analogues.

I regard providing an opportunity for formulating strong sensory impressions into words as very important, as it helps to establish a semantic basis for these memories that can allow them to be stored in archived memory and fade away from recent memory. This prevents later intrusions, as the memory loses its "here and now" quality, and will be more difficult to retrieve. The process of verbal overshadowing also occurs. Research experiments have shown that attempts at a verbal description of a picture actually decrease the ability to identify the picture (Schooler & Engstler-Schooler, 1990). The early opportunity to put the experience into words and put the trauma into archived memory fits well with Ehlers and Clark's (2000) cognitive model of PTSD. This model emphasizes: a) the need for the trauma memory to be elaborated and integrated into the context of a person's preceding and subsequent experience in order to reduce intrusive re-experience, b) the problematic appraisals of the trauma and/or its sequelae, and c) the need to reconfigure dysfunctional behavioral and cognitive strategies that prevent memory elaboration, exacerbate symptoms, or hinder reassessment of problematic appraisals. Ehlers and Clarke have developed their model with the particular aim to treat. Similar neuropsychological mechanisms support the model of debriefing in the prevention of post-traumatic confusion leading to the eventual development of long term posttraumatic disorders, such as PTSD, depression, anxiety states, and substance abuse.

As I describe in more detail later, it is very important for leaders to handle this part of the debriefing with great care. If it is the case that only a few participants have been exposed to strong sensory impressions, a detailed review of these participants' exposure may traumatize non-exposed participants. Group composition (only exposed participants) or direct leadership (not focusing on sensory details) can guard against untoward consequences of the group process.

The Reaction Phase

Questions about thoughts often lead to answers filled with preformed emotional content. The expression "I thought I was going to die" vividly expresses both fear and helplessness. For this reason, the thought and reaction phase are often intertwined. **When handling this phase it is important to remember to:**

- Allow participants to talk about themes of central importance.
- Follow the time-sequence (immediately, afterwards, and now).
- Cover behavioral reactions, somatic reactions, and feelings.
- Accept reactions without dwelling on the individual.
- Inquire about the worst part of the event.
- Use and mobilize the group for support, if needed.
- Visit the "unspoken" emotions.

During this part of the meeting, participants are allowed to talk about themes of central importance for their experience. They may talk about emotional reactions such as anger, fear, guilt, sadness, and helplessness. Some of these themes may have already become apparent when they described what happened to them, or they may also have surfaced during the thought phase. To make a workable structure for their expression it is useful to ask participants about reactions in a time sequence. **A valuable exercise can be to ask how they reacted while the situation was unfolding, then about reactions immediately afterwards, and then reactions that have ensued in the following time period. Besides emotional reactions, bodily, or somatic reactions, behavioral changes they have noticed can be inquired about at this time.**

If participants react with strong emotions during the meeting this should be looked upon as normal and reactions should be accepted without dwelling too long on that participant. There may be a compelling temptation to do that, but it is a mistake. The group can be used to support members physically, for example, by holding or hugging and by soliciting their verbal support. Strong experiences are often associated with powerful emotions. Most people have the capacity to control their situations once they have ventilated these emotions, and they are able to regain a sense of perspective, balance, and equanimity over time. How to deal with difficult emotions will be outlined in more detail later.

Do not be afraid to inquire about the worst part of the experience for the participants. It is by being able to give words to these aspects that some of the power of these events may be reduced and more control can be gained. This can be asked about in the following manner: "What was the worst part of what happened for you?" "If there is one part of what happened that you would like to erase from your memory, what would that be?" or "When you look back on it now, what part of the event was the hardest one for you?" If strong emotions emerge during the meeting, use and mobilize the group members to support each other.

If there are themes of importance that the group members do not bring up on their own, it is the group leader's task to ask about this in a gentle manner. By asking, the leader also conveys the naturalness and normality of having had certain thoughts or reactions, something that in itself can be helpful and increase a sense of empathetic understanding.

Leaders may make concrete inquiries about stress symptoms that the participants may have experienced both during and following the event but might not have mentioned. However, care needs to be taken not to over-focus on problems or symptoms that might create self-fulfilling prophecies or even make the participants believe they *have* to have these symptoms in order to be normal. The best method is always to ask open questions and then focus on those reactions that most of the group have actually experienced to some degree, collectively, such as sleep problems, increased fear, or heightened bodily arousal.

The Normalization Phase

When the participants have talked about their most important thoughts and reactions, the atmosphere in the group changes. For instance, laughter in the group emerges, there are more body-movements and restlessness, and the participants start looking at their watches and signal that they want the meeting to come to a close.

These group signals should be detected by the leaders and responded to. **It is time for the leaders to comment on some of the presented thoughts and reactions. In the normalization phase the issues to remember are:**

- Review and comment on presented thoughts and reactions
- Describe types and expected course of reactions and give advice on when to seek help
- Provide general and specific advice concerning:
  — Stress management
  — Expressive strategies
  — Control strategies
- Provide written information[2]
- Give time for questions

---

[2] Appendix B contains an example of a leaflet that can be handed out to a group.

The introduction of the normalization phase can be done with the following statement: "It seems to me that you have described many important aspects of your experience and the thoughts and reactions that have accompanied these experiences. Before we end this meeting there is some information we want to convey and some advice we would like to give you." Following this introduction, the group leaders comment on how the thoughts and reactions they have heard are normal reactions to abnormal situations, and similar to those expressed by others. The group leaders can normalize further by pointing out how such reactions are common following adversities such as those that the participants have gone through.

There are good reasons to wait for the normalization phase until the end of the debriefing approaches, as this allows the participants to hear the common thoughts and reactions of others first, before an attempt is made by the leaders to wrap things together. By having the normalization phase late in the meeting, the group is already learning how others think and react for themselves and they are not simply "told how to react." Unfortunately, it is not uncommon for debriefings to be held where "experts" come and tell a group how they are reacting and what they can expect in the time that lies ahead.

Following a train disaster, emergency workers were "debriefed" by mental health professionals from a local hospital without much experience of disaster or debriefing work. They were told how to react and what they could expect. In interviews with the press, the workers complained that they were treated like psychiatric patients and "talked down to." They did not need an expert to tell them how they were reacting. Being a mental health professional is no guarantee that one knows about debriefing, and proper training is necessary to prevent debriefings that "make thing worse," as was the perception of some of the participants in these debriefings.

Depending upon the time that has passed since the participants experienced the trauma, the group leaders go on at this stage to describe the anticipated normal course of such reactions and give them advice on when and where to seek help.

In some situations the debriefing leaders should provide psycho-educational material before the normalization phase. I recommend this when:

· There is little chance that the group members will normalize the response.
· When somebody makes a statement that will hold the group back: "I do not think it is right to react like that."
· When there is a good chance of explaining or interpreting a response for the group's best.
· When it allows feedback on responses from several group members.
· When it keeps the discussion/conversation moving.

I think that in the near future we will provide Web addresses where the participants can access specific self-help advice for common problems. Psycho-educational aspects have always been part of debriefing, but I foresee a more specific use of such measures. Important advice should be outlined involving activity that can decrease tension, counteract avoidance, lower intrusions, and facilitate the transition to meaning over time. Those who become more passive when facing stress may continue to experience stress-effects over longer periods of time as compared with those who are more expressive. As Gal & Lazarus (1975) reported, individuals get considerable relief from symptoms by "forcing" themselves to engage in activity following intense stress. It is important to note that it is not the actual control of the situation, it is the feeling of mastery that the person gains from the action he is performing that reduces his anxiety and feeling of helplessness (Gal & Lazarus, 1975). In this way, symptoms can be viewed as having considerable potential for positive adaptation, at least in the initial phase of reaction to a trauma.

A debriefing meeting in itself is a kind of activity that may have helpful effects by engaging participants in a ritual that provides social support, and a sense of control and structure in an otherwise troubling situation that is also often chaotic and unstructured. This can play a significant role in regulating the emotional state. Psychoeducational aspects of the debriefing, with suggestions to members on how to actively deal with the situation at hand, can be a powerful tool in improving the participants' sense of control. Self-helpfulness replaces helplessness.

Advice On Seeking Further Help

When a debriefing meeting is **conducted within the first week** following a traumatic situation, the following guidelines can help with regard to when a person should seek further assistance:

- If strong reactions continue over the first 3 to 4 weeks without showing any sign of declining.
- If reactions increase instead of decrease over time.
- If a person has a strong sense of unreality, of not being himself or herself.
- If a person is unable to function in his or her ordinary life (socially, occupationally, or in other important areas of functioning).
- If a person undergoes very marked changes in personality.
- If a person starts self-medication, i.e., by drugs or alcohol.

When a debriefing meeting is held after a longer interval some different guidelines can be added. For example:

- If reactions have lasted over a month and contain strong intrusive material entering a person's thoughts, and there is strong evidence of avoidance of situations, persons, and conversations that invoke memories of the traumatic event; feelings of detachment and a sense of foreshortened future; and strong and sustained hyperaroused body (c.f., definitions of a posttraumatic stress disorder–PTSD).

· If the person is markedly depressed or overanxious. Remember that ordinary grief does not require treatment, but if a person has suffered a traumatic loss it may result in complicated grief. Complicated grief is characterized by reactions similar to the ones mentioned above, and include frequent efforts to avoid reminders of the deceased, feeling stunned, dazed, or shocked, experiencing purposelessness or feelings of futility about the future, having difficulty acknowledging the death, lost sense of security, trust and control, and excessive irritability, bitterness, or anger related to the death.

· If reactions increase instead of decrease over time.

· If a person is unable to function in his/her ordinary life (socially, occupationally or in other important areas of functioning).

· If a person undergoes very marked changes in personality.

· If a person starts self-medication, i.e., by drugs or alcohol.

Some other risk signs that may increase the chance of developing long-term problems are:

· Exposure to grotesque death

· Having lost a child

· A high degree of life-threat

· Having undergone torture, intimidation, or rape

· Previous psychiatric problems, especially "neuroticism" or having the tendency to see things in a gloomy or depressive way

· Lack of adequate support systems

· Strong sense of responsibility for what happened and excessive guilt feelings.

The use of screening, both during the debriefing and then at the follow-up debriefing, provides a very important possibility to identify people in need of individual follow-up. Some authors have advised against immediate services for all "victims" (Bisson,

Jenkins, Alexander, & Bannister, 1997; Brewin, Andrews, Rose, 1998), suggesting monitoring symptoms to pick up cases at one month post-trauma, a strategy less likely to engage people in follow-up unless initial contact has been made earlier. The non-stigmatizing and non-psychiatric approach involved in debriefing allows a mental health professional to build rapport and establish competence and confidence in a manner that makes it less "dangerous" to accept individual help when it is appropriate. As almost all participants are receptive to debriefing and report a positive experience, enhanced compliance with subsequent interventions could follow. When debriefings are used as part of a crisis intervention approach, survivors of critical and traumatic situations are in an enhanced state of psychological "prepared-ness" for further help, if that is required, and resistance to receiving such help will be reduced. The use of screening measures, for example, the Impact of Event Scale (Horowitz, Wilner & Alvarez, 1979) or similar measures, are helpful instruments that can ensure that appropriate help is provided for those in need.

> *Following a maritime disaster, all survivors were asked to fill in the Impact of Event Scale and the General Health Questionnaire (Goldberg, 1978) (as well as answer other questions) around 1½ months following the disaster. Based on their scores, those above a recommended cut-off score that indicates danger for PTSD or other mental health problems were contacted individually and offered further help.*

During the last decade, new trauma-treatment methods have proven effective in reducing problems induced by critical events. Solomon (1998) has advocated the early use of Eye Movement Desensitization and Reprocessing (EMDR) in crisis situations and together with Jeffrey T. Mitchell has started to use it for those who show strong reactions after debriefings. Within the Federal Bureau of Investigation, EMDR has been tried out shortly after CISD and is claimed to "have a very powerful and rapid effect" (McNally & Solomon, 1999). Until more data are available,

I would recommend against moving in too quickly with therapeutic procedures. People should first have the opportunity to use coping strategies that they were able to learn during the debriefing meeting, or the natural fading away of reactions following a critical event should have an opportunity to be effective. Therapeutic interventions may be unnecessary. However, if a person continues to show problems at the follow-up debriefing (or if contacted about a month after the event), there should be little hesitation in starting more active therapeutic procedures. If there is evidence of very strong reactions leading to significant impairment (e.g., Acute Stress Disorder), there should be no hesitation in moving into therapeutic regimes using EMDR and other techniques.

Advice On Coping

Regarding how to cope with these reactions, here are some helpful self-help strategies that can be advised:

· Give words to the experience.
· Seek out facts to get a cognitive grip on the situation.
· Get information about usual reactions.
· Use music, rest, physical exercise, and relaxation to reduce tension.
· Be careful of increased intake of coffee, sugar, alcohol, and nicotine.
· Try to keep up the daily routine as much as possible.
· Use prayers, religious rituals, and other cultural self-help and self-soothing strategies.

Activity seems to be especially important for individuals in stressful situations and can be highly effective in reducing threat and distress. This also makes the psycho-educational aspects of the debriefing, with suggestions to members on how to actively deal with the situation at hand, a powerful tool in improving the participants' sense of control. Important advice should be outlined involving activity that can decrease tension, counteract avoidance, lower intrusions, and regulate and help in the transition to meaning over time. Those who become more passive in the face of stress may continue to experience stress-effects over a longer period of time.

If participants have experienced intrusive images of their trauma, it can be helpful to ask them to set aside some time during the day when they can actively bring this intrusive material into consciousness so that they can attempt to process and manipulate it in their mind. This can also be done as a prevention strategy, especially if they have taken in strong sensory impressions, providing them with a self-help method they can use if the memories become a problem later. If it is a visual image that keeps returning, they can imagine seeing this on a screen and then imagine having a remote control where they can press the off-button to remove the images. They can also imagine having a video player attached to the screen and when they start the movie with the unwanted images, they can press the recording button, record the images, and then stop the recording. Then they can imagine taking out the fantasy video and lock it away in a drawer. They can also be advised to call up the image and try to push it further away until they can barely see it any more.

If they hear sounds or voices, i.e., screams, they can imagine hearing them from a radio and then turning down the volume by the use of the volume control. If it is an intrusive smell, the advice is to put some nice-smelling oil in their nostrils to replace the bothersome smell. Such techniques help the person regain control over these images, sounds, or smells instead of the reverse.

If people experience great fear for certain situations, the best advice will be for them to gradually expose themselves to what they fear until they can gain more control over this fear. Usually the use of relaxation or deep breathing through the nose a few times will help relax the body and make it easier to confront the situation. By taking one step at a time, combined with relaxation, people can regain control and reduce fear. This approach to graduated exposure (successive approximation) is predicated upon the principle of reciprocal inhibition. The interested reader should refer to Meichenbaum's (1977) text on cognitive behavioral therapy.

If people are bothered by nightmares, I recommend going through what happened in a detailed manner while awake. Nightmares are like "flashbacks at night" and if the flashback material is encouraged to present itself by day and attempts are made to process it, it is less likely that it will appear at night. A new "happy ending" can also be added to the nightmare. Another technique that has proven helpful for nightmares is to write down the nightmare in detail immediately after being awakened by it, before trying to sleep again.

It is helpful to provide some written information about normal reactions in this phase and allow time for questions.

The Closure and Future Planning Phase

Before closing the meeting, the group leader will ask if there are any additional issues that the participants want to bring up or discuss. The issues to cover are:

- Any additional issues?
- Focus on group learning and the future
- Make appointment for a follow-up debriefing if necessary
- Inform about available follow-up resources
- Immediately following termination, contact "risk" participants
- Be present for a while after the meeting

If there are no additional issues, it is important that the leader makes a short summary of some of the discussion that has taken place during the meeting. The emphasis is on what participants have learned about the normality of reactions and especially on how they may have learned new ways of understanding the situation or dealing with their reactions. They are asked to assist each other in remembering the advice and guidance, and motivated to help each other in dealing with what has happened. It is helpful for a group to end on a positive note. However, some debriefings take place following situations where the group has experienced the loss of one or more of their friends or co-workers, where it would be disrespectful to try to create such a positive focus. I try to create a positive outlook whenever it is appropriate, as it broadens the group's attentional focus and behavioral repertoire and thus their overall resources. Sometimes it is appropriate to use positive reappraisal or cognitive strategies for reframing a situation to see it in a positive light. For example, you could say, "I know that most of you definitely would not have wanted to be part of what happened, but as long as you were, look at what you did to survive. All of you contributed in some way to the fact that you are now sitting here safe and sound. By your thinking and actions, you were able to stay alive. For the rest of your life, you will know that you have the resources to act in a critical situation and for many of you present here today, this event will help you to keep in mind what is important in life and what is not."

Although it may be too early for participants at the debriefing to interpret a negative event in a positive way, for many the creation of positive meaning is possible. This is parallel to what Folkman and Moskowitz (2000) term situational meaning, involving creating, reinstating, or reinforcing meaning in the midst of stress. Such processes can be very strong and positively "contagious" in a group. The leaders' challenge is to make use of spontaneous remarks from the participants that reflect such creative and constructive thinking or carefully introduce it when participants do not bring this up. This is most easily done with the event more at a distance and will be a very important part of the follow-up debriefing.

Often it is important for groups to make firm commitments to meet again at this point and this may be suggested and arranged. The debriefing leader makes the suggestion about whether or not to meet again based on the nature of the incident and its consequences and what has been observed and reported during the meeting. If a follow-up debriefing is to be held, arrangements for this are made (i.e., setting the date and place).

The debriefing leaders should state that they will be present after the meeting to be of assistance if anyone wants to share something that was hard to disclose in the presence of the whole group. Depending upon the individual follow-up opportunities, the group leaders may give information on where those who are in need of more help can get such help.

At the very end of the meeting, it is important to praise the group members for sharing their experience and for the way they have supported each other during the meeting. Following some meetings there may be a "ritualized" ending by the group sharing a meal or doing something together.

At the end of the meeting, participants considered being "at risk" by the leader should be contacted to arrange for individual follow-up. This contact is less stigmatizing if the co-leader initiates it. This is also the appropriate time for debriefing leaders to make arrangement for those group members whom they detect to be especially traumatized or affected by strong sensory impressions.

Follow-Up Debriefing

Some events are so powerful that the need for a follow-up debriefing is clearly evident at the first meeting, while at other times it is unclear how much this is needed. If this is unclear, the participants or the group leader can be contacted after some weeks and a decision can be made regarding the need for a new meeting. The need for a follow-up debriefing is usually greater in groups with no training or background for handling a traumatic event, thus making follow-up debriefings more rare among professional helpers. Even among professional groups, however, a disaster involving a great loss of life or an especially emotionally charged event such as the unanticipated death of a child, may make a follow-up meeting necessary.

If a follow-up debriefing is to be held, I advise setting it up four to five weeks following the first meeting. The follow-up debriefing is not as structured as the first debriefing. Basically the leader welcomes the group, shortly restates some of the rules and then asks the group if any new facts about the traumatic event have become known since the last meeting. Sometimes it is advisable to have someone with intimate knowledge about the event come to the follow-up meeting to convey facts (i.e., a physician, an investigator, a pilot following an air-crash) to augment what is already known and to reinforce the underpinning factual structure of the critical incident.

After new facts are discovered, participants are asked about how things have been since the last meeting. It is advisable to use a timeline for this; for example, first ask about how it was in the first week, then afterwards, and finally how it is now. Thoughts, reactions, and behaviors are covered and hopefully, by using this timeline, the participants recognize how they have returned towards normal functioning. Busuttil and co-workers (1995) have described a "lines exercise" during which participants plot out a time-graph of their lives in their own personal journals. All significant positive and negative events, including the traumatic stressor, are plotted on the vertical axis, while time (age) is plotted on the horizontal axis. The main aim of this exercise is to identify positive and negative coping strategies. Although originally used as an integral part of the 12 day, in-patient course for the treatment of PTSD, the "lines exercise" could be adapted for use as a concrete way of eliciting coping mechanisms in the case of ordinary follow-up debriefings.

It is important to let the group exchange practical suggestions on how they have handled the situation and reactions resulting from the event. Coping advice from within the group has the best potential to be used by participants. The debriefing leaders can supplement this advice, and also answer questions that arise.

Following a maritime disaster where many lives were lost, several of the survivors, who comprised the debriefing group, gathered for the follow-up debriefing and complained about sleep problems. Apart from the possibility to refer those in need for individual follow-up, they were advised on sleep hygiene as well as instructed in several specific sleep induction techniques.

In the follow-up, it is also possible to inquire sensitively about knowledge or growth that has resulted from the critical incident. If the group is a team or a natural work group try these questions: What have they learned about helping each other? How can they apply their new knowledge to other difficult problems or situations they may face as a group? In what way can they make use of the new learning, for example, in working out new procedures or plans? If this is a group of people who were strangers before the critical situation, how can they be of continued benefit for each other? What have they learned about their own resources? Did they become aware of previously hidden strengths? Are there any lessons to be learned, knowledge to be gleaned, or plans to be made for the future?

For the re-entry phase, it was mentioned that one should seize the opportunity to learn from the acquisition of new coping skills. This becomes even more important during the follow-up debriefing. Perception of growth and learning about how to master difficult situations help to boost confidence for the future. This goes for both individual and group learning. Critical events have the potential to shape people's lives both negatively and positively and the leaders' tasks are to help the group to gain from the event and make sure that the potential for positive reappraisal, growth, and constructive changes in held values are optimized.

The follow-up debriefing is an excellent opportunity for identifying people in need of individual follow-up. Besides motivating them for making contact if they feel the need themselves, it is possible to make contact with those participants that the debriefing-leaders identify as still struggling with the effects from what has happened. At this point, screening measures can be handed out to be returned by mail and, upon return, be analyzed to secure further help for those in need.

5

The Defusing:
Meetings on the First Day

While a psychological debriefing takes place several days following a critical incident, a defusing is a meeting undertaken on the same day as the incident. When working with crisis incidents, it is obvious that many people will have a strong need to talk about what happened directly afterwards. A defusing allows for a semi-structured way of doing this. In helper groups, this may sometimes be the only meeting undertaken, while in community groups, a defusing meeting will often set the stage for the later debriefing meeting. The goals of a defusing are mostly similar to those of the debriefing, but in addition it secures an early opportunity to muster or re-establish a social or collective response and ensure that people do not isolate themselves from each other. It also makes it easier to decide whether or not a full debriefing is necessary.

There are similarities and differences to the debriefing. The difference is related to the structure. Since people at this point usually have not taken in all the emotional ramifications of the event, they can be stunned, dazed, or still "in action" mode, and it will be inadvisable to force them through a structured debriefing. There is also less capacity at this stage for taking in information about usual reactions and the provision of normalizing information is thus kept brief. However, there are usually similarities to debriefing in that there is a short introduction and the mentioning of some rules, as well as some structure to the talk-through before short advice is given toward the end of the meeting.

Practical Aspects of Defusings

There is less time for organizing this meeting and therefore one has to adapt to the circumstances at hand. Some characteristics of defusings (adapted from Mitchell and Everly, 2001) are:

- Groups are usually small
- Used within the first eight hours of the event
- Duration usually short, maximum 90 minutes
- Environment needs to be free of distractions
- The purpose is similar to the debriefing
- The meeting can eliminate the need for a debriefing
- A defusing can make the debriefing process easier to undertake.

The meeting is often held in close physical proximity to the event and participants will be those who were affected by the event. An outside team, for example, from occupational health organizations, HMOs, leaders, or others from the affected group who were not involved in the event will lead it. The meeting should preferably take place within the first 8 to 12 hours of the event. Some people might need individual assistance and should, of course, be provided with such assistance.

In work teams within the military and in different emergency responder groups, it is usually the ordinary team leader or trained peers who will lead such a meeting (if he/she has not been part of the incident). Although the training of the leaders or peers does not have to be as rigorous as training before conducting a formal debriefing meeting, it is strongly recommended that those who are to undertake such meetings do not do this after having only read an article or a book. It seems so easy when one reads about it, but in reality it can be both complicated to lead and sometimes involve strong outpouring of emotions. In many countries, such as the U.S. and Australia, there have been many peer supporters within different emergency services that have achieved training to handle defusings—a tradition less strong in other countries. Even in the services where peer support persons receive formal training to lead defusings and be co-leaders/leaders in debriefings, a formal debriefing will not be undertaken without the presence of a mental health professional. This testifies to the more complicated nature of a debriefing compared to a defusing. Turnbull (1997) describes a carefully planned and clinically sensitive approach undertaken to debriefing prisoners-of-war and hostages. The requirement for debriefers to have a professional mental health background and highly developed clinical skills in such situations is obvious.

As soon as possible after the event, it is usually important that affected persons can call home to notify their loved ones about what has happened, as many events receive media attention that may leave those at home worried.

It is recommended that defusings take place in smaller groups of six to eight people. This is easy to achieve in emergency responder groups where natural team groups can be used. However, in other critical situations, groups may be larger as the affected work or community group is of a larger size. If not too large, it is advisable to keep the group together.

Although Mitchell and Everly (2001) state that these meetings should take 20 to 45 minutes, I have found that they often last longer, especially when dealing with non-emergency responders. When provided with a defusing, bank clerks often will spend 1 to 1½ hours talking following a bank robbery. Participants with training and experience and who previously have participated in a defusing may require shorter meetings. Flexibility in the approach, such as allowing the group the time they need, will have to govern our use of time in these situations.

Especially among helper groups, a defusing may be what the group needs to get a grasp on what happened and get the necessary talk-through, i.e., following a surgical operation that went wrong. The early chance to go through what happened and place it in perspective may be enough to get a grip on the event and no further meetings may be required. If the event is of a magnitude where a debriefing is called for, the defusing often starts the process of setting words to the event and showing the group the benefit of this.

Although the same person does not have to lead both the defusing and debriefing, the group can benefit from the same leadership. Meeting the group during the defusing will result in the participants already having trust in the familiar leader and being more willing to invest in the debriefing meeting.

The structure of the defusing meeting is:

- Introduction
    — State purpose, motivate
    — Review rules
- Exploration
    — Review what happened
    — Discuss what happened
    — Talk about facts, thoughts and reactions
    — Assess the need for further help
- Information
    — Provide information about reactions
    — Normalization
    — Offer advice on coping
- End
- New meeting?
- Follow-up resources

It is evident that defusings and debriefings have similarities in structure. Defusing meetings are less structured. Defusing starts with the leaders introducing themselves and giving a short description of what the meeting will be about. Mutual support is encouraged, as is participation, before the need for confidentiality is emphasized. If there are any preliminary questions, they are addressed. After this short introduction, what the members actually bring up will become the focus of the conversation. The leaders ask their questions based on cues from what the participants bring to the forum. There is no order as to who should speak, but everyone is invited to contribute by the leader's verbal or non-verbal behavior. Usually there is a great need to speak, so that conversation flows easily and moves smoothly from one theme to another. However, just as in the debriefing, it is the leader's task to make sure that no single participant has to take undue blame or be the target of anger from the others. Instead, it is the leader's task to make sure the group is steered in such a way that it is not destructive for any individual members or indeed for the entire the group.

During the information phase of the meeting, the defusing team briefly summarizes the information that the group has provided and answers any questions that the group may ask. Experiences and reactions that emerge are normalized and common, immediate reactions are mentioned. For example, following bank robberies, I usually inform groups that it is not unusual to feel anxious after returning home and that they might feel a need to lock the door and draw the curtains. Some experience difficulties in falling asleep or restlessness; or some may shiver or sweat more than usual. It is pointed out that these reactions are temporary and will soon fade away and also that it is not necessary to experience such reactions to be normal. Following this, some simple advice is given on self-soothing or tension reduction strategies. Groups are advised to collect someone else around them to comfort or talk to them, to refrain from drinking too much coffee or using other activating substances, and to do what they have found helpful to reduce stress or tension before. This advice is limited to a few minutes, and can in addition be made available in a short handout leaflet.

During the defusing meeting, the leaders evaluate the need for a formal debriefing and if this is deemed necessary, a time for this is communicated to the group before they leave. The defusing team stays on after the defusing to make sure that any participants in need of more assistance have their needs attended to. It is common for one-on-one consultations to follow a defusing. These often reflect private concerns not easily aired within a group, or sometimes people show evidence of very strong reactions for which an individual focus is required.

6

Leadership in Debriefing Groups

Good leadership reduces the possibility of a negative outcome. There are a variety of tasks for a leader in a debriefing. He/she needs to:

- Quickly establish an atmosphere of trust
- Outline goals and motivate the group for participation
- Build relationship to the group and its individual members
- Be a role-model for the group
- Choose, address, clarify, and time important issues
- Build cohesion and support within the group
- Guard against destructive group-processes
- Assess strengths and vulnerabilities in participants
- Stimulate and fine-tune a positive group process

To reduce or prevent some of the negative effects mentioned previously, skillful intervention is needed by the leader. Throughout the meeting, clear leadership is shown. At some points it is active and at other points it is passive, but at all times the responsibility rests on the leader for directing and facilitating the group process. There may be lengthy periods during which the group members talk to each other without leaders playing much of a part, but leaders are there to stop any destructive processes or take charge when certain themes need closer exploration. Leader activity usually declines over time, as the group members start to exchange information about thoughts and various reactions and then it increases again towards the end of the meeting. Once into the process, the more the members address each other and not the leader, the smoother the group is running.

A debriefing leader must have a thorough knowledge of crisis reactions, especially of mental mobilization, to be able to understand the reactions of individual participants and the group, and know how to and when to use this knowledge in relation to the group in focus.

An example illustrates the importance of leaders conveying information:

> *During and following a discotheque fire that killed 63 young people in Gothenburg in 1998, survivors and bystanders strongly criticized emergency responders for arriving too late and doing too little. Their anger was strong enough that it resulted in physical clashes with the rescuers. During meetings for groups of young people afterwards it was extremely important to convey information about how fire-rescue personnel go about their job and the difficulties that they experience in an operation such as this. But it was also very important to give an explanation of the altered time sense that took place in the situation. This is part of the mechanism of mental mobilization that usually helps us survive. In this situation it was vitally important that they had an understanding that it was their own subjective sense of the rescuers taking a very long time to arrive, and not the actual time the rescuers took that was the basis of their anger. A special task force from the fire service met the young people and their explanation about mental reactions was conveyed as well.*

Gerry Larsson and colleagues (Larsson, Tedfelt, & Andersson, 1999) have reported on a qualitative study of debriefing leaders and debriefing participants. Based on their article, I have summarized some of the variables they have highlighted as essential qualities of high-quality, secure debriefing leaders:

- Basic personality characteristics
  — being calm
  — being flexible
  — being stress tolerant
  — having good self-awareness
  — having basic technical knowledge
  — having academic training in behavioral sciences
  — having knowledge of group dynamics
  — having knowledge of crisis dynamics
  — having ability to identify individuals with complicated reactions
  — having thorough knowledge of debriefing methodology and working conditions of the affected group
- Emotional leadership
  — good empathic ability
  — ability to sense the needs of the individual group members as well as the group atmosphere
  — honest interest in the group members
  — courage to confront strong emotions
  — sense for how much space he/she should occupy as a leader

From the findings of Larsson and colleagues, it is evident that no matter how much training we provide to future debriefing leaders, there are some characteristics, such as a secure inner self and a good empathic ability, that cannot easily be gained through training. We may have to be more selective regarding who we provide with training in conducting these meetings.

Larsson and co-workers have also pointed out some of the important aspects of secure leadership in groups:

- The quality of debriefings are formed in dynamic interplay between the group and the debriefing leader characteristics.
- The debriefing leader must instill faith, confidence, and security.

- Secure leaders give a detailed presentation of the session as well as of themselves.
- Secure leaders ask for more detailed descriptions from the participants.
- Secure leaders appear able to confirm and normalize strong reactions.
- They have an ability to use silence to activate impressions and fantasies and leave time for participants to have their say.

First of all, they point to the process or interplay between leader and participants. The climate established inside the debriefing room depends upon characteristics of the group and leaders. Larsson and co-workers then go on to mention critical leadership qualities to instill confidence, to motivate, to facilitate, to confirm, and to normalize the participants' story. Their findings are very much in line with what I have written elsewhere (Dyregrov, 1997b, 1999). During the meeting the leaders act as a model for participants regarding:

- Directness
- Honesty
- Respect
- Encouragement
- Enthusiasm
- Vitality

When the leaders are quickly able to establish a climate of trust and respect and at the same time build up the participant's motivation to invest in the process, the debriefing meetings have a high chance of being successful in helping members to learn as much as possible about the event, process their thoughts and emotions, and integrate what they have been through. Much depends upon the leaders' ability to handle the **introduction** well, if the meeting is to go well. The introduction is where the climate and the process get off to either a good start that will positively help the group members, or to a poor start that will impede the group process. Aveline (1993) wrote that: **"What happens early on powerfully shapes later events"** (p. 112). This is true for both individual therapy and for groups. The tone of the meeting is set in the first six to ten minutes. The introduction, with its focus on rules and structure, shows participants that there is clear leadership and a clear procedure to the ensuing process. This lowers anxiety and enables participation. However, participants can experience too much structure as a negative feature (Rohde & Stockton, 1994). Leaders have to create a balance between structure and flexibility that facilitates participation. Usually, it takes time to build trust and establish the climate necessary for members to talk easily about their experiences, thoughts, and reactions. In debriefing groups, the climate that facilitates everything that is to take place later is established by the leaders during the introduction phase. This must be done in such a way that members feel comfortable about sharing their inner experiences. Essential trust is built by the way that leaders present themselves, the purpose of the meeting, and the rules.

Trust and authority are built and based upon a combination of non-verbal and verbal communication. It is formed by the way the leaders use their eyes, by what they say, and the manner in which they say it. The leaders must be able to look at the members, move their eyes from side to side during the introduction to include all members of the group, and then change focus and give total attention to each group member during the fact-phase. By their investment of energy in the group, the leaders will determine how much the members will invest in the ensuing process. An unprepared leader without the power to motivate or focus the group on its purpose will not be successful. If the leaders do not "take" the necessary authority in the group and establish the group rules, they will have little control over how the group deals with more difficult themes, emotions, and conflicts later on.

A group may be anxious and insecure at the start of the meeting and group leaders need to be able to deal with this and make the group feel at ease. When situations of group insecurity arise during the meeting, for example, when conflicts surface, Larsson, Tedfeldt and Andersson (1999) note that personality characteristics (see previous page) of the leader and their ability to handle group dynamic processes appear to be even more important than the technical skills of debriefing.

How to Lead the Group Process

Experienced leaders know how to feel the "pulse" of the group. For those with less experience it is helpful to start as a co-leader in the beginning and then move on to be a leader as experience increases. Over time, a leader will learn more about:

- Noticing who gets attention in a group
- Noticing the themes of importance in the group
- Anxiety and defensive mechanism (negativism) in a group
- How to read eye contact and other non-verbal signals between participants
- The meaning and function of laughter in the group
- Cohesion and conflict in groups
- Interruptions
- Changes in group climate

To facilitate the group process, the leaders have to be able to "read" the group. They must be able to feel and understand the "pulse" of the group, notice who gets attention in the group, register the themes of importance, interpret the meaning of pauses, and understand and handle any anxiety or defensive mechanisms in the group. In addition, eye-contact between the members, laughter, cohesion and conflict, interruptions, and changes in group climate over time will all provide the leaders with input that may influence or determine the direction of the meeting. These represent many, sometimes complex, tasks that take a lot of energy out of the leaders, as well as demanding an expert understanding of processes involved.

By paying attention to such aspects and learning to read the signals, a group leader can steer the group process optimally.

These skills take time to develop. By getting feedback on personal handling of different themes in a debriefing meeting and from discussion with other group leaders, the leader-in-training's knowledge is gradually increased. If somebody mentions something that others have obviously also thought or experienced, the leader can say: " Are there any others who have reacted in a similar manner?" or "Has anyone else similar thoughts?" Short facilitations with minimal "lecturing," interpretations, and feedback will be beneficial for the group. Participants will feel that it is "their meeting" and assume responsibility for its process and the conversation will run smoothly. Leaders need to monitor the verbal and nonverbal cues that the group participants provide constantly, to facilitate the process. The interaction between the leaders and the participants, and the participants with other participants, ensures a smooth flow of information at a conversational level that stimulates a vigorous group process.

With experience, the leader will add an intuitive quality to his/her work. Intuition is characterized by rapid use of previously accumulated insights from the following sources:

- Subliminal perception
- Non-verbal cues
- Body posture
- Tonal qualities
- Eye contact
- Group movement

Intuition also means the ability to rapidly understand perceptions or symbols that originate in the inner world and the metaphors and images that describe his/her experience. This leads to a sense of "just knowing" or "gut feelings" about another person's thoughts and mood state.

To have that intuitive sense of knowing is probably not something that can be achieved by training alone, but giving undivided attention to another individual or a group will help it to develop, so that the "figure and ground" can be seen at the same time (see each participant and the whole group).

By intuition and accumulated knowledge a debriefing leader may:

- Feel the "pulse" of the group
- See the gestalt of the group process
- Sense the patterns that are emerging, i.e., the group movement
- Know what strategies to employ
- Know when to be quiet.

7

Stimulating Group Processes and Group Movement

It is important to remember that the group exists for the benefit of group participants and not for the leaders to "show off" how much they know. This means that following the introduction and the fact phase one should try to:

- Keep leader interruption to a minimum by short facilitations:
  — "Are there others who reacted in a similar manner?"
  — "Are there others who had similar thoughts?"
- Encourage group activity
  — use one's eyes, hands and feedback from the group to steer and further stimulate group interaction
  — make links between different contributions
  — keep interpretations and "lecturing" to a minimum.

Asking short questions helps to keep the group active, as it encourages group participation and "keeps the ball in their court." Long leader sequences inhibit group activity. Comments that facilitate group activity are: "Have any others reacted in a similar manner?" "Did anybody else have similar thoughts?" "Tell me more." "Does anyone want to respond to this?" and similar responses. To clarify, ask: "Could you explain this a bit more?" Group leaders make great use of their eyes and hands, and feedback from the group steers the whole process. If anyone should nod their head when an important theme emerges it indicates that they are in agreement. The leader can look at the person who nodded immediately and be quite sure that the person will shortly have something to say.

Short, active-assisting gestures by the group leader, such as responding to the nod, means that the participants will have to take the initiative more often. Therefore it is important to keep interpretations and "lecturing" to a minimum. Although the group leader may want to show off how much he/she knows about crisis and trauma reactions, this will usually interfere with the group process in a negative manner. By leaning towards the person who speaks, nodding, and "modulating" one's eye contact, varying one's tone or voice, by adjusting one's head position and use of hands, the group leader can stimulate and regulate the activity of the group participants. If the group participants are eagerly exchanging opinions or experiences, the debriefing leaders can lean back and let the flow of the conversation continue and make their presence felt as little as possible. However, they have to keep track of the conversation very closely to know precisely when there might be a need to step up the steering process.

The leader should intervene or take charge to fine-tune or stimulate the process when:

- Destructive processes are erupting.
- The group is ready for a new theme.
- The group becomes preoccupied with one issue.
- The group loses its focus and starts to engage in "small talk."
- There is an opportunity for the participants to validate somebody's comment and the group refrains from doing this automatically.
- The group becomes preoccupied by some historic point which is not directly relevant to the "here and now."

Bridges between phases should be kept short and they often can come naturally. Sometimes they have to be forced because of time pressure. It is a great temptation to summarize the proceedings too much and too early. The cost is loss of the natural rhythm of the group. Again, it is important to remember that the leader's task is simply to facilitate the group, and not to illustrate how much they know about psychological reactions to trauma. Mostly it is about listening, which is an active role and not a passive one.

Respected leaders, who are attentive to the participants, provide verbal and non-verbal feedback, are open and honest, and are attuned to what is happening in the group, foster a good group climate. The leaders must be able to find the right balance between activity and passivity, between individual and group focus, and they have to develop the skill of fading out discussed issues and amplifying newly introduced ones. The focus is on issues of collective interest, not on those particular to some individuals. However, if the leader does not acknowledge these individual issues, albeit briefly, the impact on the group process can be negative and impeding.

Summarizing by the group leaders themselves should be greeted and used with caution as it has the potential to halt the process quite abruptly. It may be fruitful to use when:

- The theme has been discussed at length and starts to recur (by summarizing one can move to the next theme).
- A theme is introduced before the last one was settled.
- One needs to help engage those who have not been involved in conversation.
- One phase is ending before moving on to the next phase.

Summarizing even at the end of a phase should be kept short to prevent interruption of the flow of the process. Otherwise, it can act as a dam.

Seating positions and the quality of rapport with each individual group member help to create a climate that can significantly improve the prospects of success. Further, if the leader behaves as an expert rather than as a facilitator and repeatedly interrupts the flow of conversation, the process is slowed down or halted. Affirmation of a group member's reactions must come from the other group members, not from the leader. However, when members raise highly significant reactions not easily affirmed by the others, the leader needs to be able to make a contribution to catalyze further conversation and group commentary. Knowing when to do what and why demands a comprehensive awareness of common reaction to crisis and trauma.

Negative Group Traditions

I have discovered it is easy to become "stuck" with some unproductive habits that can so easily develop in a group meeting. One such habit or "tradition" is going around the group from member to member several times. This can easily be interpreted as a demonstration of rigidity and obsessive behavior, and discourages free interaction and interplay between group participants. It is also very easy to focus too much on the facts to the degree that the other dimensions of the event are not covered adequately. The leader's task is to make sure those all-important aspects of the critical event are given the necessary amount of time to be processed.

Group leaders have to ensure that the group "tradition," in which members feel under pressure to disclose aspects of their experience that they otherwise would not have talked about, does not develop. Over-disclosure can be a real problem, but preventing resistance is probably more difficult to deal with. This aspect is discussed later.

Raising Themes Not Raised By Participants

The complexities of debriefing meetings become evident when leaders have to address the themes that participants do not raise themselves. It is, however, not simply their prerogative, but is also their responsibility to do so.

Some years back I met a group of colleagues following

a suicide attempt by one of the group. The individual succeeded in becoming paralyzed from the neck down. The group struggled with guilt because although they were able to talk openly about the event, nobody managed to raise the issue of "maybe it would have been best if he died." When this theme was sensitively raised by the debriefing leader, it obviously was an important one for them to be able to share both in terms of thoughts and feelings.

Debriefing leaders have to be aware of issues that are important for the group to talk about but that they find difficult to raise. These issues have to be handled with sensitivity but nevertheless they need to be talked about, especially with groups that are to continue to work together or interact in the future in an effective way.

Aveline (1993) has argued that the leader's task is to attend to the unattended. By observing when a group "nerve" is touched and by using previous and present experience and knowledge, the leaders have to coordinate the discussion of important themes for the group with flawless timing, whether the members raise the themes or the debriefing leaders raise them. This fine-tuning of the group, as to how fast or slow to move, how deeply to explore the themes, when to change the theme, and when to move on to a new phase, represent the skills of group leaders. They are of supreme importance. Without the proper "feel" for the group, understanding of the process, and authority to steer it, the group is in danger of losing much of its beneficial potential.

8

Negative Experiences in Groups

The Nature of Negative Experiences

Negative experiences or unsuccessful groups can be a reflection of a number of factors. The characteristics of the participants in a group, the group's leadership, aspects of the group's environment, and properties that evolve within the group are all crucial factors. **Among possible negative consequences are:**

- Exposure to traumatic details; secondary traumatization
- Open conflict between members
- Competition between team leaders
- Domination of the group by one member
- Incorrect or inappropriate feedback regarding facts, normal reactions or coping strategies
- Mishandled group process, i.e., blaming, guilt

Although there is no reason to think that many of these dangers are characteristic of most debriefings, their existence should make us aware of the respect we should have for what we undertake when leading such meetings. For this reason I provide some advice on how to handle such experiences should they arise.

To illustrate the danger of secondary traumatization, two examples are described:

A policeman was killed in the line of duty. One police officer, at that time in therapy for other problems, reported that being part of the debriefing following the *line-of- duty death had been very negative for her. She had not seen the dead body, but the detailed description by a colleague upset her very much. It brought back all the memories she faced following the situation that brought her to therapy. The leaders had taken on **an over-heterogeneous group**, where members exposed to strong sensory impressions were allowed to describe their impressions in too graphic detail.*

Another example illustrates how this can be handled to prevent harm:

I worked with a group following an explosion that killed two members of a work group. The sensory-exposure involved taking in graphic details that I won't even try to convey here. In the debriefing group that met to talk this through, there were some members who had absorbed all the gory details, while others were not present at the exact place where it happened. To prevent intrusive recollections it was very important that those exposed to the sensory impressions were given an opportunity to give the sensory fragments a verbal form as is normal. However, doing this in detail within the group would pose a risk of traumatizing other members of the work group. The debriefing group was originally planned to include those exposed to the situation, and this mixture of exposures came as a surprise for us as leaders. We decided to request those without the strong sensory exposure to wait outside while we focused on these aspects, and then they were invited in again.

The risk of contagion exists when members vividly describe their experiences. When the whole group has similar experiences, the possibility for harm is reduced. However, with only some members describing highly distressing memories and experiences, others may be at risk for visualizing or imagining what others describe in fantasy form. Such fantasies can in themselves take on an intrusive nature. Tehrani (1998) has recommended that the focus should be on the factual content of what has occurred and that engaging in emotions should be "avoided." I think we will miss important opportunities by observing such a restriction. However, care is needed if strong emotions are to be engaged and embraced as an integral part of the group process. Leaders without the proper training, experience, or sensitivity can easily mishandle such an event. The use of homogeneous groups will decrease the risk of harm or hurt in this respect.

During the first days following a critical event, a narrative or story about the event will develop among group members who have been exposed to the same incident. Different perspectives, observations, and experiences are woven into a coherent story, which in the end becomes the group's mutual story. This story or version is not necessarily a "true" or objective story, but the consensus story. However, as Shalev, Peri, and Rogel-Fuchs (1998) have pointed out, such versions may alienate those who experience incongruent observations, feelings, and thoughts. The leaders have to guard against undue pressure that might be felt by individuals to conform to the consensus story and explain to the group how different perceptions will arise in critical situations. Sometimes there will not be "one" story, but several, and the debriefing leaders need to kindle respect for different perceptions of the same situations.

A bomb-like object was thrown into a social welfare office and several members of the work group came rushing to the scene from their rooms within the larger office to see what was happening. Three of them happened to come at about the same time. All three claimed to be the first ones in the room, and their attention had been so focused on the "bomb" that they did not see the others arrive. There was no point in trying to build a single cohesive story, but it was possible to make the point that perspective in such situations becomes very focused, and they had all contributed towards the rapid evacuation of the office.

Drawing on aspects from mental mobilization, they could then see for the first time how well they had handled this event as a group and they turned their attention to exploring other issues of the situation. The "sticking-point" had been overcome.

I believe that the major objections against debriefings are based upon the fear that they will trigger a process whereby the individual searches for symptoms that he/she has heard from others or from the debriefer (in effect, a self-fulfilling prophecy). Both Matthews (1998) and Carlier et al. (2000) have drawn attention to the danger that involvement in debriefing may intensify workers' stress response or their perception of stress. The psycho-educational component draws attention to individual reactions and can take on a form of self-fulfilling prophecy or lead to the expectation that one should have certain symptoms to be normal. This can lead to higher levels of stress, in addition to the fact that negative moods are more contagious than positive. Again it will be the leaders who will have to facilitate the group in such a way that such processes are guarded against. It is extremely important to make sure that the psychoeducational information does not convey to people that they need to have certain reactions to be normal. By participating in the group, an individual can learn new ways to express feelings, thoughts, and impressions which were not previously part of the usual repertoire as well as benefit from other aspects of the debriefing previously noted.

Handling Difficult Situations

Although the format and structure for such groups seems simple and straightforward, it is important that group leaders are aware of some of the dangers that can result from debriefing groups. In addition to the problems mentioned earlier, difficulties may arise because:

- Members may find too much self-disclosure threatening
- Members may become overwhelmed by listening to other people's trauma

- When too much is disclosed too soon, some participants become "anxious"
- Some participants may experience a sense of helplessness
- When "everything" is accepted as normal, people who are in need of individual help may hesitate to get the help they need
- Some participants may be in danger of "taking" over other people's distress and despair
- A high degree of cohesion in the group can lead to pressure on other group members to conform and have similar reactions
- Some important topics that need to be discussed may never be raised.

To prevent such problems it is important to follow the structure, as this moves the whole process in a smooth manner from facts to thoughts and then on to reactions. Naturally in this way there will be less over-disclosure at the outset, and participants can relax before more painful material is discussed. Almost everyone can and wants to share what happened to them, and most people can talk about their thoughts. By starting the meeting focusing on facts and thoughts, many find it simple to convey their reactions later. "What happened" naturally leads to the dimension of "how do I feel about what happened" but does not work the other way around.

It is also the leader's responsibility to make sure that the rest of the group is not traumatized by the stories of the others. The telling of graphic and grotesque details represents the risk in this respect. If the suggestions made earlier in this book are followed, this can be prevented. If group members put pressure on others to behave or feel in a certain manner, it is also the group leader's task to make sure that there is room for individual reactions and opinions.

Group members may not raise some topics because they are too painful. It is very important to bring up these topics and to talk about them in a sensitive manner. Some of these can be brought to light by the group leaders. Usually such sensitivities can be earmarked by skillful ways of starting the discussion, by saying, for example: "I know that what I am now going to bring up is a painful theme for many of you, but painful themes are often some of the most important themes to discuss. I would therefore like to ask you ...."

Other problems in debriefing groups can be:

- Participants that are unwilling to contribute
- Members that hide behind facts and intellectualizations
- Open conflict between members
- Excessive silence
- Judgmental statements.

If participants are unwilling to contribute it usually results from too little time and attention being paid on the introduction to the meeting. By creating a good climate for the meeting, the problem then becomes having enough time to discuss all the issues that the group wants to focus on and definitely not that people do not want to say anything. However, if there is one member who the others distrust, or the group is uncertain on how the information will be used afterwards, they may refrain from investing in the process. It is therefore important to establish a good climate by making sure that people feel safe and that they know that what they say will not be misused or misrepresented.

Some members are only able to talk about what happened in a distanced, remote, and impersonal manner and should not be pressured towards showing emotions. It is the individual member's own responsibility to decide how much they would like to say and how to say it. The gradual evolution of the group process will often reduce the tension, and participants may become more personal in their descriptions.

Conflict in the Group

The following can summarize some general rules concerning how to handle conflicts:

- Try to relax physically and not become drawn into the conflict
  - — Monitor your own words (beware of an aggressive tone or phraseology)
  - — Beware of accusing members
- Try to be constructive
  - — Try not to make anyone lose face in front of the group
  - — Do not enter into long arguments that will exhaust the group (be brief and direct).

Conflicts can be handled by other tactics as well:

- Acknowledging and dealing with the conflict
- Clarifying the issues by eliciting pros and cons for the different positions.
- Finding possibilities for a compromise position
- Allowing disagreement – explaining "different" memories, how the event can be remembered differently depending upon focus of attention
- Temporarily setting aside or postponing the issue
- Paying attention to "losers" in conflict situations
- Acknowledging that there is a conflict, but that the group is not the best forum for resolving it
- Remembering that unrecognized conflict becomes a hidden agenda that interferes with group interaction.

If there is open conflict between members of the group, it is important that this conflict is acknowledged and dealt with openly. Unrecognized conflict becomes a hidden agenda that interferes with group interaction. It is the leader's responsibility to protect members against intimidation, coercion, threats, and undue pressure. If there is conflict, it is important that the debriefing leader tries to relax physically and carefully avoids aggressive or patronizing tones. The leader should try to be constructive and not make anyone lose face in front of the group. Long arguments will tire the group, and so it is important to be both brief and direct.

The best way of handling conflict is to try to clarify the issues involved by having the participants make their positions clear and to try to establish both sides of the argument. If there is a possibility for a compromise, seek it out and see if the two conflicting individuals or sides can be drawn into an agreement. Allow for disagreement and explain how different perceptions or memories of the same situation can exist in parallel as participants focused their attention on different aspects of the situation. In this way it is possible for group members to understand that they can have different views of a situation without one person being more "right" than another, or one person being completely "right" and the other one totally "wrong."

If it is clear that the issue cannot be solved or settled in the meeting, it is important to put the disagreement to one side and try to find ways to deal with it afterwards. If, despite the best of intentions, there remains a "loser" or "losers" in a conflict situation, they should be closely monitored during the rest of the meeting and may need special attention afterwards. Remember that conflict is a spur for change that is often necessary for development and that it can actually be a powerful motivation for the realization of goals in the whole group.

Sometimes there is an awareness ahead of the meeting that serious conflicts exist and going ahead with a debriefing group may not be advisable. The presence of authoritarian individuals among the group to be debriefed or the presence of current psychopathology among members should also lead to caution about using a group format for helping participants.

Handling Intense Emotions and Anger

If intense emotions emerge during the meeting the following suggestions may help to handle them:
- Allow expression if the emotion is directed outside the group (i.e., anger); the tension will usually decline with verbal expression.
- Assume control and set limits for expression if it is directed at members of the group.

- Use reflection on the process: "I wonder if some of this anger/blaming reflects the helplessness one feels when ..." or "I am not quite sure what this is about when I hear all of your blaming ...."
- Allow arguments to be set forward in a controlled fashion (see above).
- If emotions reflect old conflicts, extract the issue out of the group. Provide suggestions for whom they may contact to solve them.
- Remember that truth can be difficult to accept during heated conflicts.
- Reframe the anger and acknowledge that when a person is angry at someone, this usually means that this person is important to the other.

If intense emotions of sadness, guilt, or self-reproach surface, the following advice can be of help:

- Allow expression to alleviate the reaction
- When possible, use the group to support
- Normalize by using the group when the reaction is common
- Normalize from the leader position when the reaction is unusual
- Ask what the group members think or feel about what a person says.

Allowing the expression of these emotions will usually alleviate the intensity of the reaction. Other group members are usually the best source of support. Simple signs, for example, can solicit their support by signaling to the participant who is sitting beside someone who starts crying to put their arms around the individual, or ask other participants what they think or feel when they observe him/her crying. It is also possible to say, "To me it seems like your tears are not your tears alone, but belong to the whole group." Usually this will lead to tears forming in other participant's eyes as well.

When somebody experiences an intense, common emotion, letting others describe similar reactions can also normalize it. If the experience is unlikely to be experienced by others in the group, the leader can draw on experience to normalize the experience. There is no substitute for extensive knowledge about crisis reactions. It is vital to know when to do what and what to do when.

When the group refrains from talking or discussing important issues, it is helpful to try to understand the reasons behind this. Sometimes it can be helpful to collude with the denial for a while because it is just too difficult to raise a particular issue, or it might be that participants do not feel safe with each other. By carefully closing-in on difficult issues, a conversation can be established: "I know it may be painful to talk about ...." Sometimes it is also possible to point out to the group that their reluctance to discuss a certain theme has a certain meaning, for example, "I noticed that you have talked about the facts, but you leave out some of the attached emotions and thoughts." Another intervention is to formulate a paradoxical statement: "Is there an issue that you really do not want to talk about?"

If an individual in a group expresses self-blame or guilt it is important to encourage the conversion of guilt into words and explore the underlying rationale. It is usually not helpful to intervene too abruptly and to try to console by saying "There is no reason for you to feel that way" or something similar. Usually the group will not allow one person to assume responsibility on his/her own and they will help to distribute responsibility. By specifically inquiring for the thoughts behind the self-blame, it is usually possible to gather information that makes it easy to sum up and say something like: "Based upon what I hear you say it does not seem that you had any other option at the time you made your decision." Or, "From what you say, it sounds to me that the alternatives you now see were not open or clear to you in the hectic moments when this happened, and that it is only now afterwards that you see other options. When you judge yourself you should only do it based on the options that were available to you at the time of the crisis." After hearing a person out and understanding the reasons behind the choice of action, it may also be advisable to ask the group what they think: "What do you think after hearing him/her describe the situation and what he/ she chose to do?"

The use of different cognitive methods, such as focusing on what one knew at the time of the decision, distribution of responsibility, Socratic ways of questioning, etc., are usually helpful when dealing with guilt feelings and self-blame. Although applicable in groups, most of these techniques (Kubany, 1998) are formulated for individual work, and as a debriefing leader one should be acutely aware of the need to refer those who are really "stuck" in destructive thinking.

Handling Lack of Participation

If some members of the group are "underparticipants," they can be stimulated to participate in the following way:

- Respect your own "rule" – low participation style is normal for some group-members.
- Look for " I want to participate" cues.
- Invite group members to participate " What do the rest of you think of this?"
- Praise on-topic contributions when they come.
- Use the comment, "Some of you may be reluctant to say something because you think it is unimportant, but remember...."
- Be willing to break your "rule" once.
- Remember that those who do not participate verbally may still benefit greatly from the meeting.

First of all, it is important to respect the rule about not having to say anything. Remember that low participation is to be expected in some participants. Their silent attitude may be part of a shy or "silent" personality. If some members are very passive, look for signs that they want to participate or invite them to participate for example, by saying: "What do the rest of you think of this?" If they contribute, praise them when their response is pertinent to the topic in question. It can also be useful to comment in the following manner: "Some of you may be reluctant to say something because you think it is unimportant, but remember ...." Although there is a rule that states that they do not have to say anything, it is appropriate and prudent to break this rule once during the meeting and ask an underparticipant to respond to something that he/she mentioned during the fact phase. Do remember, however, that those who do not participate verbally may still benefit greatly from listening to others present at the meeting. If silence is combined with little attention to what goes on in the group, for example, eyes fixated firmly on the floor or some other point throughout the meeting, I would contact the individual at the end of the meeting to ascertain whether or not individual follow-up is needed.

Watchorn (2000) reported that those who did not actively disclose during debriefings, especially those who had experienced high levels of peritraumatic dissociation, had experienced a greater concentration of problems over time than those who disclosed. When we looked at survivors following a maritime disaster (unpublished data) who held themselves back during the debriefing due to a perception of conflict in the group (assessed by a questionnaire) we found a similar trend. Those who kept back revealed elevated avoidance rates on the "Impact of Event Scale." Such results may help us understand some of the "underparticipants" in such meetings. If they have strong dissociative mechanisms and we as leaders are unable to stimulate active participation in a debriefing, they may run the risk of more problems over time. The challenge for us as clinicians is *when* we time our interventions to engage these people, and an even more important issue is, how do we make sure that they will actively engage in a group? With their avoidant strategies, it may be difficult to encourage them to attend debriefing meetings and to take an active part when they do actually attend.

It is a paradox that people who might be most in need of information about reactions or support from others may be those who do not turn up for debriefing meetings. Presumably these individuals either anticipate disapproval or rejection by the others, or fear that what is disclosed may add to their stress level rather than reduce it. The various motivations for not participating should make us careful about how we approach them to motivate participation in follow-up meetings. Emphatic understanding coupled with words that acknowledge their resistance can counteract their reluctance to participate. It is important to remember, however, that it is likely that many of those who do not want to participate simply do not feel a need for such meetings as they already may be on the road to recovery.

Handling Group Denial or Flight

Sometimes members of the group do not want to talk about a certain theme, or they avoid it because of the pain involved. It is important to be sensitive and make quick decisions regarding whether to respect this or, on the other hand, to see it as an escape from talking about an important issue. There is no easy way to decide when to do what. It is helpful to try to understand the reasons behind the denial or avoidance. Is the issue too difficult to raise? Does this reflect conflict in the group? Can it be a form of helpful denial, not to be tampered with? It is the knowledge of the group leaders and their ability to read the group and the situation in the right way that will determine what to do.

If the decision is to try to do something about this, it may be helpful to:

- Carefully close-in on difficult issues; *"I know it may be painful to talk ...."*
- Point out to the group their evasiveness; *"I notice that you tend to talk about the technical details, but leave ...."*
- Leave the issue for the group to chose: *"Is there an issue that you really do not want to talk about ?"*

I think we should keep in mind that debriefing reflects our Western cultural belief that talking and expressing painful events will be helpful for us. In other cultures, disclosing negative emotions and one's deepest thoughts and feelings are believed to be responsible for poor health, illness, and general misfortune. For the Balinese, it is believed that sadness spreads when it is verbally and non-verbally expressed (Georges, 1995). The only appropriate technique for the elimination of distress and the preservation of sanity and health is to not think about or not care about the experience. In this situation, laughter is regarded as especially effective, while disclosure weakens one's life force. Georges (1995) writes " ... it becomes evident that no single, universal meaning or function can be attributed to the institutionalized disclosure of intimate thought and feelings" (p. 21). Wellencamp (1995) writes: "If, for example, there are strong cultural norms that work against disclosing emotions, or if there are cultural beliefs about the danger of talking about certain experiences, these may influence the experience and consequences of disclosure, just as the presence or absence of a receptive audience may affect whether disclosure is a positive or negative experience" (p. 309). It is important to keep cultural variations in mind when we expect people to express themselves in a group.

Handling of Group Monopolists

Although it does not happen often, sometimes one comes across a person who has no feeling for the rest of the group and goes on talking and talking to the frustration of the group and its leaders. I have used the term 'group terrorist' for this, but Yalom's (1995) term 'group monopolist' is better and less derogatory.

It is important to recognize that a person may talk a lot because his/her head is so filled with or preoccupied by the event that he/she does not take in his/her surroundings at all and becomes a group monopolist. In my experience this person will best be cared for in a one-to-one relationship. During a debriefing, the co-leader may have to leave the room to assist the person. This must be done with respect and care, i.e., by saying: "I understand that this event has had a very strong impact on you and that it is hard for you to focus on what the others are saying. I think it would be best for you that you and ___ (indicating the co-leader) take some time where just the two of you can go through what happened from your perspective."

However, the more problematic participant in this category (the real group monopolist) is the person who lacks any social perception or sensitivity of taking up too much of the group's time, continues to talk in minute detail, or is very hard to interrupt. Even when asked, in the mildest and kindest way, to let others have a chance to say something, the person's lack of social sensitivity soon results in him/her taking the lead again. Although it is easy to write what one should do, in reality, it is never easy. The following advice summarizes my own methods of handling this situation and some techniques used by others:

- Introduce preventive rules
- Take notice of the non-verbal signals in the group
- Do not postpone intervention
- Do something before you become frustrated
- Start with a smile and be polite
- Let the strength in the limit-setting increase over time
- Use clear non-verbal signals as support when restraining the "monopolist"
- Selectively ignore input.

If nothing else helps, some professionals advise using the group to "correct" or comment. I would advise against this as I find that it is an abdication of the leader's responsibility. This strategy is best used in therapy groups where it is important to teach a person how his/her behavior impacts on the group, but debriefing is not therapy.

Sometimes, one participant starts his/her story about what happened and gives a rather detailed review of events. This may be a person who has a very good overview of the event and it may be very important for the others to hear the story. If one starts to view this too soon as undemocratic use of the group's time and intervenes to stop, one may actually do the group disservice. It is important to "read" the group by noticing how they listen. If they all continue to be attentive, one should let the person have his/her say. If, however, the group members roll their eyes, divert their attention, become fidgety in their seats, or look at each other (in short, disinvest their energy in the process), it may be a sign that the person's behavior is typical of how he/she always monopolizes the group.

When one has to intervene, it is very important to do this in a respectful and caring manner. Refer to the rule about the democratic use of the group's time; do it with a smile and know that you will probably have to do it again. If you are too "hard" or authoritative the first time around, you may lose the group. A group will never allow one of its members, however annoying he/she is, to be treated unkindly or disrespectfully without some repercussions for the leadership. In a debriefing group, you run the chance of the participants de-investing in the process. The first mild "correction" will help you build your mandate to be more "strong" or authoritative the next time around.

It is my experience, the few times I have had one of these monopolists in a group that you always lose some of the group's momentum. Because of the negative influence, the group may not be as successful as it could have been without the monopolizing.

When is it Not Advisable to Conduct a Debriefing?

Based upon common sense and the problems described above, it is not advisable to conduct a debriefing when:

- Strong conflicts exist in the group ahead of event
- Very authoritative workgroup leaders are present
- There is much psychopathology among members
- Participants are too tired
- The timing is wrong
- Key people are not present
- There is an absence of group need for the intervention.

These are some aspects that should lead to caution regarding the use of debriefing. If, however, one attempts to use the procedure, it does require a high degree of professional background and experience.

Care For Group Leaders

Conducting debriefing meetings can be very demanding and exhausting for the debriefing leaders. The energy spent on being attentive and listening to participants describe traumatic material, while at the same time mastering the group process, take a heavy toll on concentration and use of mental energy. For this reason, it is important to run sessions with a minimum team of two in order to properly handle problems or conflicts as they arise. This also provides the important element of someone to talk to following the meeting regarding what happened. By investing sufficient time on preparation for the teamwork and planning how to do the introduction, the chance of a successful debriefing is increased.

Debriefing leaders should know each other well before the meeting and set aside time for talking through the experience following the meeting. These post-debriefing meetings are an important way of protecting the team and should include: a) a review of what happened during the debriefing to learn what took place, b) a way to make sure that different tasks concerning follow-up of individual members are properly distributed, and c) a chance for "ventilating" how the debriefing was experienced by themselves to ensure that any distress is reduced.

If debriefers are exposed to very strong stories, it may be advisable to hold a debriefing meeting for the debriefers. Talbot (1990) has described the parallel processes involved in debriefers following their involvement. She points out how the debriefers' experiences (feelings, thoughts, and behaviors) are similar to those encountered in the debriefing participants and that this can affect therapeutic interventions. She proposes making sense of these parallels to give meaning and structure to our work by supervision and follow-up meetings for debriefing leaders. Together with colleagues, she has described a debriefing of the debriefer strategy and the processes involved in this strategy (Talbot, Manton, and Dunn, 1992). Turnbull (1997) describes what he calls "support" or "secondary debriefings" for debriefers involved in debriefings of prisoners-of-war and hostages to manage the "ripple-effect" of emotional contamination experienced in such arduous work.

Providing effective "helping the helper" routines is important and some of the same self-help suggestions presented earlier in this book should be utilized to ensure care for the debriefing personnel themselves. These meetings are so demanding that the number of successive sessions led by the same debriefers during a single day should be restricted.

Readers are also referred to other books for a closer examination of the cost of helping and strategies for ensuring the health of the debriefers following traumatic or critical situations (Figley, 1995; Pearlman & Saakvitne; 1995; Saakvitne and Pearlman, 1996).

9

Into The Future

As we gather more research on the effective components in debriefing, we will probably see changes to the procedure. One of the changes that is easy to predict will be the development of more trauma-focused group treatments following larger accidents and disasters. While debriefing groups can be used for large groups of survivors or other prioritized groups affected by the disaster, more focused groups can then be organized for those screened and found to be in need of more help one month after the disaster. These focused trauma groups base their work on trauma therapeutic principles already in use for children and adolescents (March, Amaya-Jackson, Murray, & Schulte, 1998; Smith, Dyregrov, Perrin, & Yule, 1998; Turner, 2000).

In the future, I think that we will learn more about how to refine and develop debriefings. There will be a better fit between the type of group to be debriefed and the debriefing process involved. This is especially true since debriefing groups are no longer restricted to emergency responders, but used for primary victims as well. Groups of primary victims do not have the training and experience of professional helpers and thus these groups will contain people with more varied backgrounds. Such groups will need more experienced leaders to handle the problems that may arise when members have a more heterogeneous background and exposure.

Another change I foresee, which is already being implemented, is to develop more specific guidance to participants on how they handle specific after-reactions following crisis events. Direct instrumental and confrontational coping shows a positive relationship with health probably by improving the sense of control and by providing better problem solving (Paez, Basabe, Valdozeda, Velasco & Iraurgi 1995). During debriefing meetings I have conducted over the last few years, I have instructed participants on specific techniques that they can use to take control over intrusive images. Likewise, when participants at follow-up debriefings complain of sleep problems, they get specific advice on different strategies they can use. Such specific guidance can be given in written form, but some verbal instructions may often be needed.

Another change that I foresee is a better understanding of the persons that do not benefit from such group meetings. Several researchers have found that the power of the word, linking emotion to the verbal system, is not without its risks. To benefit, the person must be able to bring together the powers of the symbolizing process and the verbal system to reorganize emotional schemas rendering them more vertical and adaptive in current life (Bucci, 1995). Shalev (1996) contends that: "Some individuals, by virtue of their coping style, may do better when allowed to repress and forget their trauma" (p. 212). One of the greatest dilemmas in early intervention is whether to intervene when people use a coping style of denial or are "blunters" that tend to use and benefit from distraction in response to stressors. What do we do when the consequence of repression is the subsequent development of increased physical and psychological illness? Should we work to include these people in groups to prevent those psychological defenses often associated with disease to continue? Should individual follow-up be instigated or should they be left alone? Although I am not in favor of mandatory debriefings, I think there is a challenge to try to involve highly defensive subjects in groups or individual follow-up in a way that does not harm them.

A number of researchers have shown that individuals who use inhibitory (repressive) coping strategies in the face of stressful life events exhibit increased objective health problems and they avoid seeking help for personal difficulties. Although defensiveness in the long run is associated with potentially deleterious consequences (i.e., decreased immune efficiency), people develop defensive emotional styles as an adaptive mechanism that supports mental, physical, and social health at least in the short term. This poses a dilemma, as we would like to involve high defenders in debriefing to secure their long-term health. However, at the same time there is research that is consistent with the hypothesis that defensiveness serves to protect one from psychopathology (Schwartz and Kleine, 1995). Schwartz and Kleine (1995) raise the possibility that defensiveness, and thus inhibition, is a prerequisite for the appearance of mental and emotional health. There is reason to believe that our practice will become more refined regarding group composition as our knowledge in this area increases. We need to tread cautiously when survivors do not want to learn more than they already recall, as they may rightfully anticipate that they will be distressed by other people's accounts when learning of further detail.

Paez and co-workers (1995) ask: " When is confronting (i.e., expressing, talking, and analyzing) a harmful effect and when is it adaptive?" (p. 208). As an answer to this question, they postulate that thinking about the problem is adaptive (improves negative affective state) when it is action oriented. Paez and co-workers (1995) also point to the timing as an important element related to the functional or dysfunctional role of inhibition and con-frontation. I think we have a lot to understand regarding how painful themes need to be addressed during debriefing-meetings, and when they are best timed.

Rimé (1995) has pointed out that natural social situations are not likely to offer people opportunities to verbalize in-depth and at-length the feelings experienced during an emotional episode. He writes: "It may thus be that what people evidence as social sharing behaviors in everyday life would rather be uncompleted attempts at processing episode-related, emotional information. One can probably conclude that in the field of emotion, there is ample place for professional intervention" (p. 287). Ritualized follow-up sessions, such as debriefing meetings, may be necessary to help process critical events.

Much research in the last decade has demonstrated a relation between dissociation and PTSD. By providing an early opportunity for calibrating the mental apparatus and getting in touch with emotional and cognitive reactions, debriefing may prevent a continuation of a dissociative reaction. The problem we face is that there may be great individual differences in the tempo of assimilation of distressing experiences which make it difficult for all the participants to benefit from debriefing at the same time.

Conducting a debriefing session is not an easy task. It has the potential to benefit and to help people following adverse events. However, to realize its positive potential and to reduce the potential to do harm, leaders must be knowledgeable and well trained. Most of all, they have to be respectful of the participants they meet.

Debriefing Procedure — Short Form

1. Introduction
   - Presentation of debriefing team
   - Stating the purpose; motivating the group
   - Rules
     — Do not have to speak
     — Emphasize confidentiality and mutual respect; no notes taken, no report written
     — Democratic use of the group's time
     — Discussion and support—not blame
     — Equal importance, no rank
   - Overview of what is going to happen (map of the terrain) and time allocation
   - Questions?

2. Facts
   - Ask for name, where they were when it happened or how they learned about it (if a death, what was their relationship to the diseased?)
   - Role in the event or at the scene
   - What did you do?
   - Rotate around group or follow time sequence
   - Factual review of what happened
   - Contextual and complicating factors

3. Thoughts
   - What were your first thoughts (if emergency personnel, thoughts and expectations while responding)?
   - Thoughts during and right after the event
   - Thoughts later and now
   - Focus on mental mobilization or important decisions reflecting adequate coping with event

4. Impressions (only when appropriate, i.e., group has all been exposed to similar stimuli)
   · Review each sense at a time, let participants chose which channel to start with
   · Let participants set words to different elements of their sensory impressions – help putting words to dimensions of sensory experience

5. Reactions
   · What was the worst part?
   · Explore emotional, behavioral, bodily and social consequences during, right after and in the time following the event
   · If one element could be eliminated what would it be?
   · Symptoms are not the most important, but providing a frame for feeling normal even though reactions were or are present
   · What effect is the event having on them now?

6. Normalization (teaching)
   · Point out commonality in reactions
   · Short description of mental mobilization strategies, usual reactions and usual course of reactions – provide written material with more detail
   · Make sure to mention that no reactions are also normal
   · Provide simple advice on coping (also in writing)
     —Rest and time to recover
     —Exercise
     —Use strategies that have been helpful in the past
     —Talk to others, use social support systems (including peers)
     —If reactions continue or intensify, or dysfunction results in work or family, seek help (mention where help can be found)
   · Make sure to emphasize positive expectations for recovery

7. Ending
  · Discuss what participants can do or tell themselves to assist their coping
  · Provide information
  · If appropriate, focus on growth, collective learning, and implications from the experience
  · Answer questions, i.e., "what ifs" and other concerns they may have
  · Remind group of confidentiality
  · Future planning with new meeting if necessary
  · Thank the group for attending and for their contribution
  · Be around for individual consultations

An Example of an Information Leaflet

REACTIONS FOLLOWING TRAUMAS AND LOSSES

Atle Dyregrov, Ph.D.
CENTER FOR CRISIS PSYCHOLOGY
Bergen, Norway

Individuals who witness or experience critical or traumatic incidents are exposed to life threat, extreme images, and strong impressions. Exposure to such events commonly leads to a range of psychological reactions that should be regarded as normal reactions to events beyond usual experience. A description of the most frequently encountered reactions follows together with advice on how to cope with them. It is very important to emphasize that it is also perfectly normal not to experience any of these reactions.

Feelings of Unreality

During or following the incident, many people experience feelings of unreality. It feels unreal, like a dream, or like something that did not really happen. This feeling of being disconnected or "in shock" actually helps us to get through the first period of time. Critical incidents often lead to a change in the perception of time. Sometimes it feels as if it is standing still, which allows us time to handle events and to make decisions and face the threat. Sometimes it feels as if it is rushing by because the mental apparatus is mobilized and the senses are sharpened so that we can deal with the threatening situation as well as we possibly can. However, the price paid for this heightened ability to take in as much as possible about what is happening is that sensory impressions can be "burnt" into memory with great detail and intensity. For many, emotional reactions are postponed by the shock, while others almost immediately experience a range of strong emotional reactions. Some people experience limited reactions both initially and later and some none at all.

Shortly after exposure to one or more critical events, a variety of reactions may be experienced. Physical reactions, such as shivering, stronger and faster heartbeats, feeling sick, becoming dizzy and feeling cold or hot, are common. Feeling helpless, overwhelmed, frightened, or sad are characteristic emotional reactions that occur shortly after the event.

However, it is often only after enough time has passed by to digest or think about the incident that emotional reactions occur. The following reactions are among the most frequent:

Intrusive Images

After being exposed to the critical incident, the strong sensory impressions that have been deeply imprinted into memory can return by forcing their way back into consciousness just as if the incident was happening all over again. Intrusive re-experiencing of what was seen, heard, smelt, touched, or tasted can be like a video-replay and are called "flashbacks" and are one of the most common after-reactions following critical incidents or dramatic losses. Sometimes, recollection of what happened takes the form of recurrent thoughts that can be very persistent. Often, these images or thoughts occur at bedtime and lead to sleep disturbances and nightmares. Shortly after exposure these memories can be very troublesome because it is not possible to control them or get rid of them.

Fear and Anxiety

Increased anxiety and arousal is another common reaction to critical incidents and losses. Fear can be triggered by anything that acts as a reminder of the event or loss, or it may be felt as a more general anxiety and fear that another "disaster" will strike. The comfortable feeling of being safe and secure that existed before the event is shattered. The increase in anxiety can be accompanied by a feeling of constant alertness or being "on guard." Increased jumpiness and exaggerated reactions to sudden noises or movements are common. The anxiety can also lead to physical reactions such as increased bodily tension, increased perspiration, digestive problems, etc.

Irritability and Anger

Another common reaction is increased irritability and impatience. This reaction is made worse by lack of energy and sleep-difficulties, and is often directed at those held responsible for the events experienced. Unfortunately such reactions also become directed at loved ones, and tend to affect close family relationships and friendships.

Sadness, Guilt and Self-Reproach

If a family member, colleague, or friend has been killed, sadness and grief will be very apparent but these emotions can also be felt even though the lost person was a more distant acquaintance. Grief reactions typically take time to sort out and may continue long after others have started to come to terms with the losses. Often this leads to a feeling of a lack of understanding from others.

Feelings of self-reproach and guilt also commonly occur, even when there is no reason to feel this way. "There must have been something I could have done to avoid this," or "If only ..." are common, haunting thoughts after critical incidents. Survivor guilt may be experienced if one managed to survive a situation in which others died. Sometimes people start frequently thinking about the risks that are run in life and about the short time span between life and death, and become more concerned about their close family.

Lack of Understanding

Some people experience more tense relations with their family and friends in the first period after critical events or losses. They may feel that family members or friends just do not understand what they have gone through. To avoid this feeling, it is important to share experiences with significant others so that they can better understand and provide better support by being available to listen to thoughts, impressions, memories, etc.

Returning To Normal Life

It usually takes some time to return to ordinary routines after critical incidents. Everything may feel unimportant when compared to what one has lived through. Difficulties regarding concentration and memory may also reduce the ability to work for some time. Comments or intrusive questioning from others (friends, colleagues) can be very painful, and it may be helpful to mentally prepare for questions and curiosity from others.

The duration and strength of long-term reactions varies from person to person. Some do not experience strong reactions while others have intense reactions. For some people the situation is normalized after a few days or weeks, while for others it will take a longer period of time to return to ordinary life.

When To Seek Help

If reactions continue and they interfere with the capacity to live and to work normally, contact should be made for individual follow-up. Also if reactions increase over time instead of decreasing, follow-up resources should be contacted. Through professional help such reactions can be worked-through and the risk for disturbing long-term effects prevented or reduced. It should be noted, however, that normal grief reactions following the loss of a loved one may have a longer time course that can last for longer than just a few months. Special mention has to be made of depression here because if you feel very depressed and your mood is incapable of being lifted or is actually getting worse then you should seek help just as soon as you begin to feel "stuck." Depression really holds up your recovery but it can be quickly alleviated with professional help.

Points of Advice

Some brief points of advice can be useful:

1. Accept your own reactions as normal reactions to extraordinary events.
2. It is not usually a good thing to try to avoid reactions when they develop.

3. Confronting thoughts and impressions brings about a better understanding of what actually happened.

4. It can also be helpful to seek out facts to get as full as possible a picture of what happened, usually by asking others who were also involved in the incident.

5. Don't rely on the media to supply the extra facts about what happened to fill the gaps in your experience. Because they are reporting the news at a distance, their perspective is often incomplete and can be sensationalized. It might be best to avoid TV programs and newspapers because they may cause disappointment or irritation.

Try to carry out your ordinary daily routines. Go to work, but remember that your work capacity can be reduced for some time, and that you can feel more tired that usual. Eat regular meals even if you don't feel particularly hungry. Try to sleep at the usual times.

Make sure that you have somebody to talk to. Talk about the events that took place as well as your thoughts and the impressions you gained from the incident.

It has proven very helpful to put traumas and losses into words by writing about what happened. Not only write about *what* happened, but about your innermost thoughts and feelings about the events. Address the two main questions," What happened?" and " How do I think and feel about it?"

Be careful not to take in more coffee, nicotine, or sugar than usual, because this adds tension in the nervous system. In this way you can take an active step in helping yourself. Music, rest, and relaxation can be used to reduce tension. The use of prayers and religious rituals can also be very helpful. Physical exercise helps to burn up the excessive amounts of adrenaline you will be generating.

If you are troubled by intrusive images from what you experienced, you may find it helpful to set aside some time during the day when you actively bring into consciousness these images and then start to change them around in your mind. For example, you can imagine seeing the images on a television screen and then imagine having a remote control so that you can press the off-button to take the images away. You can also try to call up the image in your 'mind's eye' and then start to push it further and further away until you cannot see it any more.

If it is sounds or voices that intrude, imagine hearing them on a radio and then turn down the volume by using the volume control, or by turning the radio off altogether.

If it is an intrusive smell sensation, put some aromatic oil in your nostrils to blank out the flashback smell.

Being traumatized almost always leads to a sense of loss of control and of being in chaos. The techniques described above help you to regain control over these images, sounds or smells, instead of them having control over you. More certainty, predictability, and control lead to more calm and the loss of anxiety.

References

Armstrong, K.R., Lund, P.E., McWright, L.T., & Tichenor, V. (1995). Multiple stressor debriefing and the American Red Cross: the East bay hills fire experience. *Social Work, 40*, 83-90.

Armstrong, K., O'Callahan, W., & Marmar, C.R. (1991). Debriefing Red Cross disaster personnel: The multiple stressor debriefing model. *Journal of Traumatic Stress, 4*, 581-593.

Aveline, M.O. (1993). Principles of leadership in brief training groups for mental health care professionals. *International Journal of Group Psychotherapy, 43*, 107-129.

Bisson, J.I., Jenkins, P.L., Alexander, J., & Bannister, C. (1997). Randomized controlled trial of psychological debriefing for victims of acute burn trauma. *British Journal of Psychiatry, 171*, 78-81.

Bohl, N. (1991). The effectiveness of brief psychological interventions in police officers after critical incidents. In J. Reese, J. Horn, & C. Dunning (Eds.), *Critical incidents in policing. Revised* (pp. 31-38). Washington, D.C.: U.S. Government Printing Office.

Brewin, C. R. (2001). A cognitive neuroscience account of post-traumatic stress disorder and its treatment. *Behaviour Research and Therapy, 39*, 373-393.

Brewin, C. R., Andrews, B., & Rose, S. (1998). *A preventative programme for victims of violent crime: A study funded by the NHSE Research and development programme.* Final Report. London: Royal Holloway College.

Bryant, R., & Harvey, A. (2000). *Acute stress disorder: a handbook of theory, assessment, and treatment.* New York: Automated Graphic Systems.

Bucci, W. (1995). The power of the narrative: A multiple code account. J.W. Pennebaker. (Ed.) *Emotion, Disclosure, & Health* (pp. 93-122). Washington : American Psychological Association.

Busuttil, W., Turnbull, G.J., Nal, L.A., Rollins, J., West, A.G., Blanch, N., & Herepath, R. (1995). Incorporating psychological debriefing techniques within a brief group psychotherapy programme for the treatment of post-traumatic stress disorder. *British Journal of Psychiatry, 167,* 495-502.

Campfield, K.M., & Hills, A.M. (2001). Effect of timing of critical incident stress debriefing (CISD) on posttraumatic symptoms. *Journal of Traumatic Stress, 14,* 327-340.

Carlier, I.V.E., Voerman, A.E., & Gersons, B P.R. (2000). The influence of occupational debriefing on post-traumatic stress symptomatology in traumatized police officers. *British Journal of Medical Psychology, 73,* 87-98.

Chemtob, C.M., Tomas, S., Law, W., & Cremniter, D. (1997). Postdisaster psychosocial intervention: a field study of the impact of debriefing on psychological distress. *American Journal of Psychiatry, 154,* 415-417.

Deahl, M., Gillham, A.B., Thomas, J., Searle, M.M., & Srinivasan, M. (1994). Psychological sequelae following the Gulf war. Factors associated with subsequent morbidity and the effectiveness of psychological debriefing. *British Journal of Psychiatry, 165,* 60-65.

Deahl, M.P., Srinivasan, M., Jones., N., Neblett, C., & Jolly, A. (2001). Evaluating psychological debriefing: Are we measuring the right outcomes? *Journal of Traumatic Stress, 14,* 527-529.

Diagnostic and Statistical manual of mental disorders (1994). *DSM-IV.* Washington: American Psychiatric Association.

Dyregrov, A. (1993). *Katastrofepsykologi.* Oslo: Ad Notam Gyldendal.

Dyregrov, A. (1997a). *Barn og traumer.* Bergen: Sigma forlag.

Dyregrov, A. (1997b). The process in critical incident stress debriefings. *Journal of Traumatic Stress, 10,* 589-605.

Dyregrov, A. (1998). Psychological debriefing—An effective method? *Traumatology e, 4:2,* Article 1. http://www.fsu.edu/ ^trauma/

Dyregrov, A. (1999). Helpful and hurtful aspects of psychological debriefing groups. *International Journal of Emergency Mental Health, 3,* 175-181.

Dyregrov, A. (2001). Early intervention—A family perspective. *Advances in Mind-Body Medicine, 17,* 9-17.

Dyregrov, A., Kristoffersen, J. I. & Müller, O. (1991). Når livet trues. *Tidsskrift for Norsk Psykologforening, 28,* 885-894.

Dyregrov, A., & Mitchell, J.T. (1992). Work with traumatized children—psychological effects and coping strategies. *Journal of Traumatic Stress, 5,* 5-17.

Dyregrov, A., Solomon, R.M. & Bassøe, C.F. (2000). Mental mobilization in critical incident stress situations. *International. Journal of Emergency Mental Health, 2,* 73-81.

Dyregrov, A., Thyholdt, R. & Mitchell, J.T. (1992) Rescue worker's emotional reactions following a disaster. In Engelman, S.R. (Ed.) *Confronting life-threatening illness.* New York: Irvington Publishers, Inc.

Ehlers, A., & Clark, D. (2000). A cognitive model of posttraumatic stress disorder. *Behaviour Research and Therapy, 38,* 319-345.

Everly, G. S., Jr., & Boyle, S.H. (1999). Critical incident stress debriefing (CISD): A meta-analysis. *International Journal of Emergency Mental Health, 3,* 165-168.

Everly, G. S. Jr., Boyle, S. H., & Lating, J.M. (1999). Effectiveness of psychological debriefing: A meta-analysis. *Stress Medicine,* 15, 229-233.

Everly, G.S., Jr., Flannery, R.B., & Mitchell, J.T. (2000). Critical Incident Stress Management (CISM): a review of the literature. *Aggression and Violent Behavior, 5,* 23-40.

Everly, G.S., Jr., & Mitchell, J.T. (1999). *Critical incident stress management. A new era and standard of care in crisis intervention.* 2nd edition. Chevron Publishing Corporation.

Figley, C.R. (1995). (Ed.), *Compassion fatigue.* New York: Brunner/Mazel.

Flannery, R.B., Hanson M.A., Penk W.E., Goldfinger, S., Pastva G.J., & Navon M.A. (1998). Replicated declines in assault rates after implementation of the assault rates after implementation of the assaulted staff action program. *Psychiatric Services, 49,* 241-43.

Flannery, R.B., Penk, W.E., & Corrigan, M. (1999). The assaulted staff action program (ASAP) and declines in the prevalence of assaults: Community-based replication. *International Journal of Emergency Mental Health, 1,* 19–21.

Flannery, R.B., Stevens, V., Juliano, J. & Walker, A.P. (2000). Past violence and substance use disorder and subsequent violence towards others: six year analysis of the assaulted staff action program (ASAP). *International Journal of Emergency Mental Health, 2,* 241-247.

Foa, E.B., & Riggs, D.S. (1995). Posttraumatic stress disorder following assault: theoretical considerations and empirical findings. *Current Directions in Psychological Science, 4,* 61-65.

Folkman, S., & Moskowitz, J. (2000). Positive affect and the other side of coping. *American Psychologist, 55,* 647–654.

Ford, J.D., Shaw, D., Sennhauser, S., Greaves, D., Thacker, B., Chandler, P., Scwartz, L., & McClain, V. (1993). Psychosocial debriefing after operation desert storm: marital and family assessment and intervention. *Journal of Social Issues, 49,* 73-102.

Freeman, K. (1979). CMHC responses to the Chicago and San Diego airplane disasters. *Technical Assistance Center Report, 2* (1), 10-12.

Gal, R. & Lazarus, R.S. (1975). The role of activity in anticipating and confronting stressful situations. *Journal of Human Stress,* 4-20.

Galinsky, M.J. & Schopler, J.H. (1980). Structuring co-leadership in social work training. *Social Work with Groups, 3,* 51-63.

Georges, E. (1995). A cultural and historical perspective on confession. In J.W. Pennebaker. (Ed.), *Emotion, Disclosure, & Health* (pp. 11-22). Washington: American Psychological Association.

Goldberg, D. (1978). *Manual of the General Health Questionnaire.* Windsor: NFER.

Hassling, P. (2000). Disaster management and the Gothenburg fire of 1998: when first responders are blamed. *International Journal of Emergency Mental Health, 2,* 267-273.

Hobbs, M., Mayou, R., Harrison, B., & Worlock, P. (1996). A randomized controlled trial of psychological debriefing for victims of road traffic accidents. *British Medical Journal, 313,* 1438-1439.

Horowitz, M., Wilner, N., & Alvarez, W. (1979). Impact of Event Scale: a measure of subjective stress. *Psychosomatic Medicine. 41,* 209-218.

Jenkins, S.R. (1996). Social support and debriefing efficacy among emergency medical workers after a mass shooting incident. *Journal of Social Behavior and Personality, 11,* 477-492.

Joseph, R. (1999). The neurology of traumatic "dissociative" amnesia: commentary and literature review. *Child Abuse & Neglect, 23,* 715-727.

Kenardy, J.A., Webster, R.A., Lewing, T.J., Carr, V.J., Hazell, P.L., & Carter, G.L. (1996). Stress debriefing and patterns of recovery following a natural disaster. *Journal of Traumatic Stress, 9,* 1, 37-49.

Kubany, E.S. (1998). Cognitive therapy for trauma-related guilt. I V. M. Follctte, J.I. Ruzek, & F.R. Abueg (Eds.), *Cognitive-Behavioral Therapies for Trauma* (s. 124-161). The Guilford Press: New York.

Larsson, G., Tedfeldt, E-L., & Andersson, B. (1999). Conditions affecting experiences of the quality of psychological debriefings: Preliminary findings from a grounded theory study. *International Journal of Emergency Mental Health, 1,* 91-97.

Lee, C., Slade, P., & Lygo, V. (1996). The influence of psychological debriefing on emotional adaptation in women following early miscarriage: a preliminary study. *British Journal of Medical Psychology, 69,* 47-58.

Leeman-Conley, M.M. (1990). After a violent robbery... *Criminology Australia.* April/May, 4-6.

March, J.S., Amaya-Jackson, L., Murray, M.C., & Schulte, A. (1998). Cognitive-behavioral psychotherapy for children and adolescents with posttraumatic stress disorder after a single-incident stressor. *Journal of the American Academy of Child & Adolescent Psychiatry, 37,* 585-593.

Marmar, C.R., Weiss, D.S., Metzler, T.J., Ronfeldt, H.M., & Foreman, C. (1996). Stress responses of emergency services personnel to the Loma Prieta earthquake interstate 880 freeway collapse and control traumatic incidents. *Journal of Traumatic Stress, 9*, 63-85.

Matthews, L.R. (1998). Effect of staff debriefing on posttraumatic stress symptoms after assaults by community housing residents. *Psychiatric Services, 49*, 207-212.

McNally, V.J., & Solomon, M. (1999). The FBI's critical incident stress management program. *FBI Law Enforcement Bulletin*, 20-26.

Meichenbaum, D. (1994). *A Clinical Handbook, Practical Therapist Manual for Assessing and Treating Adults With Posttraumatic Stress Disorder (PTSD)*, Waterloo, Ontario, Canada: Institute Press.

Mitchell, J.T. (1983). When disaster strikes.... The Critical Incident Stress Debriefing. *Journal of Emergency Medical Services, 8*, 36-39.

Mitchell, J.T., & Everly, G.S. (2001). *Critical Incident Stress Debriefing: An operations manual for the prevention of traumatic stress among emergency services and disaster workers, 3ʳᵈ ed.* Ellicott City, MD: Chevron Publishing Company.

Mitchell, J.T., Schiller, G., Eyler, V.E., & Everly, G.S. Jr. (1999). Community crisis intervention: the Coldenham tragedy revisited. *International Journal of Emergency Mental Health, 1,* 227-236.

Nurmi, L.A. (1999). The sinking of the Estonia: The effects of critical incident stress de-briefing (CISD) on rescuers. *International Journal of Emergency Mental Health, 1,* 23-31.

Paez, D., Basabe, N., Valdoseda, M., Velasco, C., & Iraurgi, I. (1995). Confrontation: Inhibition, alexithymia, and health. J.W. Pennebaker (Ed.). *Emotion, Disclosure, & Health* (pp. 195-222). Washington : Psychological Association.

Pearlman, L.A., & Saakvitne, K.W. (1995). *Trauma and the therapist*. New York: W.W. Norton.

Raphael, B. (1986). *When disaster strikes*. New York, Basic Books.

Raphael, B., Meldrum, L., & McFarlane, A.C. (1995). Does debriefing after psychological trauma work? *British Medical Journal , 310*, 1479-14810.

Richards, D. (1998). A field study of critical incident stress debriefing vs. critical incident stress management. *Journal of Mental Health, 10*, 351-362.

Rimé, B. (1995). Mental rumination, social sharing, and the recovery from emotional exposure. J.W. Pennebaker (Ed.). *Emotion, Disclosure, & Health* (pp. 271-291). Washington: Psychological Association.

Robinson, R.C., & Mitchell, J.T. (1993). Evaluations of psychological debriefings. *Journal of Traumatic Stress, 6*, 367-382.

Rohde, R., & Stockton, R. (1994). Group structure: A review. *Journal of Group Psychotherapy, Psychodrama & Sociometry, 46*, 151-158.

Saakvitne, K.W. & Pearlman, L.A. (1996). *Transforming the pain*. New York: W.W. Norton.

Saari, S., Lindemann, M., Verkasalo, M., & Prytz, H. (1996). The Estonia disaster: a description of the crisis intervention in Finland. *European Psychologist, 1*, 135-139.

Schooler, J.W., & Engstler-Schooler, T.Y. (1990). Verbal overshadowing of memories; some things are better left unsaid. *Cognitive Psychology, 22*, 36-71.

Schwartz, G.E., & Kline, J.P. (1995). Repression, emotional disclosure, and health: Theoretical, empirical and clinical considerations. J. W. Pennebaker (Ed.), *Emotion, Disclosure, & Health* (pp. 177-193). Washington: Psychological Association.

Shalev, A.Y. (1996). Debriefing following traumatic exposure. In R.J., Ursano, B.C., McCaughey & C.S., Fullerton (Eds.), *Individual and community responses to trauma and disaster. The structure of human chaos* (pp. 201-219). Cambridge: University Press.

Shalev, A.Y. (2000). Stress management and debriefing: historical concepts and present patterns. In B. Raphael. & J.P. Wilson (Eds.), *Psychological debriefing. Theory, practice and evidence* (pp.17-31). Cambridge: Cambridge University Press.

Shalev, A.Y., Peri, T., Rogel-Fuchs, Y., Ursano, R.J., & Marlowe, D. (1998). Historical group debriefing after combat exposure. *Military Medicine, 163,* 494-498.

Shalev, A.Y., Pitman, R.K., Orr, S.P., Peri, T., & Brandes, D. (2000). Prospective study of responses to loud tones in trauma survivors with PTSD. *American Journal of Psychiatry, 157,* 255-261.

Smith, P., Dyregrov, A. & Yule, W. (1998). *Children and war. Teaching recovery techniques.* Bergen, Children and war foundation.

Solomon, R.M. (1998). Utilization of EMDR in crisis intervention. *Crisis Intervention, 4,* 239-246.

Spiegel, D., Koopman, C., & Classen, C. (1994). Acute stress disorder and dissociation. *Australian Journal of Clinical and Experimental Hypnosis, 22,* 11-23.

Stallard, P., & Law, F. (1993). Screening and psychological debriefing of adolescent survivors of life-threatening events. *British Journal of Psychiatry, 163,* 660-665.

Talbot, A. (1990). The importance of parallel process in debriefing crisis counsellors. *Journal of Traumatic Stress, 3,* 265-278.

Talbot, A., Manton, M., & Dunn, P.J. (1992). Debriefing the debriefers: An intervention strategy to assist psychologists after a crisis. *Journal of Traumatic Stress, 5,* 45-62.

Tehrani, N. (1995). An integrated response to trauma in three post office businesses. *Work and Stress, 19,* 380-393.

Tehrani, N. (1998). Debriefing: a safe way to defuse emotion. *The Therapist, 5,* 24-29.

Tehrani, N., & Westlake, R. (1994). Debriefing individuals affected by violence. *Counselling Psychology Quarterly, 7,* 251-259.

Terr, L.C. (1992). Mini-marathon groups: Psychological "first aid" following disasters. *Bulletin of the Menninger Clinics, 56,* 76-86.

Thoits, P.A. (1986). Social support as coping assistance. *Journal of Consulting and Clinical Psychology, 54,* 416-423.

Turnbull, G. (1997). Hostage retrieval. *Journal of the Royal Society of Medicine, 90,* 478-483.

Turner, A. (2000). Group treatment of trauma survivors following a fatal bus accident: integrating theory and practice. *Group Dynamics: Theory, Research and Practice, 4,* 139-149.

Turner, S.W., Thompson, J., & Rosser, R.M. (1995). The Kings Cross fire: early psychological reactions and implications for organizing a 'phase-two' response. In J.P. Wilson & B. Raphael (Eds.), *The International Handbook of Traumatic Stress Syndromes* (pp. 451-459). New York: Plenum Press.

Ursano, R.J., Fullerton, C.S., Vance, K., & Wang, L. (2000). Debriefing: its role in the spectrum of prevention and acute management of psychological trauma. In B. Raphael. & J.P. Wilson (Eds.), *Psychological debriefing. Theory, practice and evidence* (pp. 32-42). Cambridge: Cambridge University Press.

Van der Kolk, B.A., & Fisler, R. (1995). Dissociation and the fragmentary nature of traumatic memories: overview and exploratory study. *Journal of Traumatic Stress, 8,* (4), 505-525.

Wagner, M. (1979a). Airline disaster: A stress debriefing program for police. *Police Stress, 2,* 16-20.

Wagner, M. (1979b). Stress debriefing–flight 191: A department program that worked. *Police Star,* 4-8.

Watchorn, J. (2000). *The role of debriefing in the prevention of PTSD*. Paper presented at the inaugural conference on Stress, Trauma and Coping in Emergency Services and Allied Professions, 11th–13th August 2000, Melbourne, Australia.

Wellenkamp, J. (1995). Cultural similarities and differences regarding emotional disclosure: Some examples from Indonesia and the Pacific. J.W. Pennebaker (Ed.), *Emotion, Disclosure, & Health* (pp. 293-311). Washington: Psychological Association.

Wilson, J.P., & Sigman, M.R. (2000). Theoretical perspectives of traumatic stress. In B. Raphael. & J.P. Wilson (Eds.), *Psychological debriefing. Theory, practice and evidence* (pp.58-68). Cambridge: Cambridge University Press.

Wraith, R. (1995). *Debriefing for children: are the techniques and processes the same as critical incident stress debriefing for adults*. Paper presented to Third World Congress on Stress, Trauma and Coping in the Emergency Services Professions. Baltimore April 1995.

Wraith, R. (1997). Debriefing for children: What is it we should be thinking about? *Traumatic grief—growing at different life stages*. Proceedings from the Joint National Conference, Sydney, May 7-10, 384-386.

Wraith, R. (2000). Children and debriefing: theory, interventions and outcomes. In B. Raphael. & J.P. Wilson (Eds.), *Psychological debriefing. Theory, practice and evidence* (pp.195-212). Cambridge: Cambridge University Press.

Yalom, I.D. (1995). *The theory and practice of group psychotherapy*. 4th ed. New York: Basic Books.

Yule, W., & Udwin, O. (1991). Screening child survivors for post-traumatic stress disorders: Experiences from the Jupiter sinking. *British Journal of Clinical Psychology, 30,* 131-138.

Index

A

B

C

Index

H

I

L

M

N

O